Weight Watchers™ Quick Family Meals

Jo Middleditch

SIMON & SCHUSTER

LONDON·SYDNEY·NEW·YORK·TOKYO·SINGAPORE·TORONTO

First published in Great Britain by Simon & Schuster, 1995
A Paramount Communications Company

Copyright © 1995, Weight Watchers (UK) Ltd

Simon & Schuster Ltd
West Garden Place
Kendal Street
London W2 2AQ

Design: Green Moore Lowenhoff
Typesetting: Stylize
Photography: Hilary Moore
Styling: Nicki Walkinshaw
Food preparation: Jo Middleditch

Weight Watchers Publications Manager: Delia Bintley
Weight Watchers Publications Assistant: Celia Whiston

A CIP catalogue record is available from the British Library

ISBN 0-671-71382-5

Printed and bound in Italy by Rotolito Lombarda S.p.A.

Pictured on the front cover: *Steak and Kidney Pie (page 26) and
Speedy Tomato, Bacon and Mozzarella Bread-stick Pizza (page 24)*

Pictured on the back cover: *Spicy Apple Strudel (page 58) and
Raspberry and Hazelnut Pavlova (page 58)*

Recipe notes:
Egg size is medium (size 3), unless otherwise stated.
Vegetables are medium-size, unless otherwise stated.
It is important to use proper measuring spoons, not cutlery, for spoon measures.
1 tablespoon = 15 ml; 1 teaspoon = 5 ml.
Dried herbs can be substituted for fresh ones, but the flavour will not always be so
good. Halve the fresh-herb quantity stated in the recipe.

Vegetarian recipes:
These symbols show which recipes are suitable for vegetarians.

$\mathcal{V}$ shows the recipe is vegetarian

$(\mathcal{V})$ shows the recipe has a vegetarian option

Contents

Introduction

No matter how much you love good food, for most of us time is at a premium. Whether you have a family, a job or simply something more interesting to do, you are probably not best pleased at the prospect of spending precious hours in the kitchen. *Quick Family Meals* has been written to solve this dilemma. With the recipes on the following pages you can create some delicious meals with a minimum amount of preparation and at the same time you can keep track of your Selections or Calorie intake (you will find both of these included with each recipe). Selections are the units of proteins, fats, carbohydrates, vegetables and fruits which, when following the Weight Watchers Programme, you total up each day instead of counting Calories. You are allowed a certain number of units in each category, depending on your age, sex and chosen rate of weight loss. In this way the Weight Watchers Programme ensures that you eat a varied and balanced diet. If you have a family, successful dieting can be a real problem. You either have to be constantly cooking a separate 'diet' meal for yourself – which leaves you feeling deprived – or you have to put the entire family on a diet, and suffer their moaning and snack attacks – which can be hard for you to resist. I have therefore written this book with this in mind, and created recipes that appeal to the entire family as well as being Calorie counted and designed to fit into the Weight Watchers Programme by using less oil, incorporating low-fat products and including plenty of vegetables. ⊗ When cooking some of the recipes you may be amazed at how generous the portions seem – which is another key to success, as we all need to feel satisfied. Volume doesn't have to mean Calories. Many of the recipes contain plenty of vegetables, which provide flavour and nutrients as well as volume. In many of the dishes the vegetables actually absorb the delicious flavours that have been added. ⊗ I have categorised the recipes into nine chapters of different types of meals in order to enable you to select a meal that suits your taste, the occasion or the available ingredients. The collection includes a number of vegetarian recipes and recipes with vegetarian variations, to cater for both the increasing number of vegetarians and those who enjoy incorporating meat-free meals into their diet. If you have a vegetarian in the family, you can simply cook the same recipe but use the vegetarian variation. ⊗ Weight Watchers has certainly been successful for me because the Programme teaches people how to have a healthy and flexible lifestyle which is easy to adopt for life – unlike a diet fad. I devised many of the recipes in this book while I was losing weight on the Programme. I use the recipes not only for everyday meal times but also for when friends come round – they cannot believe that you can eat so well and lose weight too!

Salads and Light Meals

The days when a salad consisted of a limp lettuce leaf, a wedge of tomato and a tired piece of cucumber are over. ⊕ This chapter provides a selection of really tasty and interesting salads which make use of a varied range of ingredients, including dried and fresh fruits, new potatoes, succulent prawns and tender pieces of chicken, which are tossed in a variety of dressings to create a meal bursting with flavour and texture. ⊕ The light meals included in this chapter cover hearty soups, pâtés and tempting toasts. ⊕ All the recipes are quick and simple to prepare, and will leave you with a satisfied palate.

High-fibre Salad

Serves 4

Preparation time: 12 minutes
Calories per serving: 235

Freezing not recommended

V

½ small red cabbage, shredded
2 large carrots, cut into long, thin strips
2 celery sticks, sliced diagonally
4 oz (120 g) dessert apple, sliced
2 oz (60 g) ready-to-eat dried apricots, chopped
1 oz (30 g) raisins
6 oz (180 g) canned haricot or cannellini beans, rinsed and drained
1 oz (30 g) walnuts or pecan nuts, chopped
For the dressing:
1 tablespoon olive oil
1 tablespoon sunflower oil
1 tablespoon white wine vinegar
1 teaspoon Dijon or wholegrain mustard
½ tablespoon chopped fresh parsley
salt and freshly ground black pepper

1. Place all the salad ingredients in a serving bowl and gently toss together.
2. Put the salad dressing ingredients in a screw-top jar and season well. Just before serving, shake the dressing vigorously to combine the ingredients and pour it over the salad. Toss gently and serve.

Selections per serving:
2 Fat; 1 Fruit; ½ Protein; 1½ Vegetable; 15 Optional Calories

Potato, Prawn and Avocado Salad

Serves 4

Preparation and cooking time: 25 minutes + 40 minutes chilling + standing
Calories per serving: 260

Freezing not recommended

1½ lb (720 g) small new potatoes
1 onion, chopped
1 quantity (to serve 4) Fromage Frais and Herb Salad Dressing (page 74)
1 tablespoon chopped fresh mint
½ medium ripe avocado
4 oz (120 g) large cooked peeled prawns
a selection of salad leaves, to serve
To garnish:
fresh chives or spring onions, chopped finely
½ red onion, chopped finely

1. Cook the potatoes in boiling salted water for 10–15 minutes until tender. Meanwhile mix the onion with the dressing in a large bowl, and stir in the mint.
2. Drain the cooked potatoes thoroughly. When cool enough to handle, slice them in half lengthways and immediately toss them in the onion and dressing mixture whilst still warm. Leave the potatoes to cool, then cover and chill in the refrigerator.
3. Let the salad stand at room temperature for 20 minutes before serving. Just before serving, peel, stone and slice the avocado and gently stir it into the salad with the prawns. Serve immediately on a bed of salad leaves, garnished with a sprinkling of chives or spring onions and chopped red onion.

Selections per serving:
1½ Carbohydrate; 1½ Fat; 1 Protein; ½ Vegetable; 10 Optional Calories

Roasted Pepper Mediterranean-style Salad

Serves 4

Preparation and cooking time: 25 minutes + 30 minutes chilling
Calories per serving: 185

Freezing not recommended

𝒱

I like to serve this salad either with 1 oz (30 g) french bread to soak up the delicious dressing or with 3 oz (90 g) cooked bulgar wheat. Remember to add 1 Carbohydrate Selection and 80 Calories per serving.

1 large green pepper
1 large yellow pepper
1 large red pepper
4 spring onions, chopped
4 plum tomatoes, quartered
4 oz (120 g) feta cheese, diced
For the dressing:
1 garlic clove, crushed
1 tablespoon olive oil
1 tablespoon sunflower oil
1 tablespoon white wine vinegar
1–2 tablespoons chopped fresh basil leaves

1. Preheat the grill. Place the peppers on a baking sheet and place it under the grill, turning the peppers frequently until the skins are charred and split. Allow them to cool.
2. Peel, core and de-seed the peppers, and cut them into thin strips. Place them in a bowl with the remaining salad ingredients.
3. Whisk together the dressing ingredients and stir the dressing into the salad. Cover the bowl with clingfilm and chill for at least 30 minutes before serving.

Selections per serving:
1½ Fat; 1 Protein; 1½ Vegetable

Tomato Garlic Toasts

Serves 4

Preparation and cooking time: 15 minutes + 30 minutes standing
Calories per serving: 195

Freezing not recommended

𝒱

Tomato and garlic is one of my favourite combinations. To flavour the toast, the raw garlic cloves are simply rubbed over it. Remember: the more you rub, the more pungent the toast will be!

1½ lb (720 g) ripe tomatoes, chopped
2–3 large garlic cloves
1 tablespoon olive oil
8 × 1 oz (30 g) thick slices crusty bread
a few fresh basil leaves or 2 teaspoons dried basil or oregano
salt and freshly ground black pepper

1. Put the chopped tomatoes in a bowl and season well. Crush one of the garlic cloves and stir it into the tomatoes with the oil. Cover the bowl with clingflim and leave to stand for 30 minutes.
2. Lightly toast the bread on both sides. Cut the remaining garlic cloves in half and rub them over both sides of the toasts.
3. Place the toasts on four serving plates, and spoon over the tomatoes. Tear the basil leaves into small pieces and scatter them over the toasts, or sprinkle the toasts with dried basil or oregano. Serve immediately.

Cook's note:
The Italian-style bread, ciabatta, which is made with olive oil, is now available in major supermarkets and is ideal for this dish.

Selections per serving:
2 Carbohydrate; ½ Fat; 2 Vegetable; 10 Optional Calories

Chicken and Rice Salad in Blue Cheese Dressing

Serves 4

Preparation time: making dressing + 10 minutes + chilling
Calories per serving: 360

Freezing not recommended

12 oz (360 g) cooked wholegrain rice
1 small red onion, sliced
6 spring onions, sliced diagonally
½ cucumber, diced
a handful of watercress leaves
1 lb (480 g) cherry tomatoes, halved
1 medium orange, peeled and sliced
6 oz (180 g) cooked skinless, boneless chicken breast, diced
1 quantity (to serve 4) Blue Cheese Dressing (page 74)

1. Mix together all the salad ingredients in a large bowl. Gently fold in the dressing until thoroughly combined. Cover the bowl with clingfilm and chill for 20 minutes before serving.

Selections per serving:
1 Carbohydrate; ½ Fat; ¼ Milk; 2 Protein; 2 Vegetable; 25 Optional Calories

Mushroom French-bread Toasts

Serves 4

Preparation and cooking time: 20 minutes
Calories per serving: 225

Freezing not recommended

$\mathcal{V}$ **If using vegetarian margarine and parmesan cheese**

4 teaspoons sunflower margarine
1–2 garlic cloves, crushed
1 lb (480 g) closed-cup mushrooms, sliced
1 tablespoon chopped fresh parsley
8 oz (240 g) french stick, sliced in half lengthways
2 tablespoons grated parmesan cheese
salt and freshly ground black pepper

1. Melt the margarine in a frying pan and gently cook the garlic for a few seconds. Then add the mushrooms, turn up the heat and stir-fry for 5 minutes.
2. Preheat the grill. Remove the pan from the heat and stir in the chopped parsley and seasoning to taste.
3. Toast the french stick halves and cut each into four equal pieces. Place the toasts on four serving plates and spoon over the mushroom mixture. Sprinkle over the parmesan and serve immediately.

Cook's note:
Chestnut mushrooms or brown-cap mushrooms are ideal in this recipe. Look out for them in your supermarket.

Selections per serving:
2 Carbohydrate; 1 Fat; 1¼ Vegetable; 15 Optional Calories

Peppered Smoked Mackerel Pâté with Wholemeal Toast

Serves 4

Preparation time: 5 minutes + chilling
Calories per serving: 290

Freezing not recommended

8 oz (240 g) skinless peppered smoked mackerel fillets
1 tablespoon lemon juice
5 fl oz (150 ml) low-fat natural yogurt
1 teaspoon wholegrain mustard
freshly ground black pepper
8 × 1 oz (30 g) slices wholemeal bread, toasted and cut into triangles, to serve

1. Break the mackerel into pieces. Place them in a bowl with the lemon juice and yogurt and mash with a fork until fairly smooth; alternatively, blend them in a food processor.
2. Stir in the mustard and seasoning until thoroughly combined and spoon the pâté into a serving dish. Cover and chill thoroughly before serving with the wholemeal toast.

Selections per serving:
2 Carbohydrate; ¼ Milk; 2 Protein

Creamy Cheese and Vegetable Soup

Serves 4

Preparation time: 10 minutes
Cooking time: 35 minutes
Calories per serving: 285

Freezing recommended

V **If using vegetarian margarine and Cheddar cheese**

2 teaspoons sunflower margarine
1 large onion, chopped
8 oz (240 g) potatoes, peeled and diced
½ leek, chopped
2 carrots, peeled and sliced
2 oz (60 g) fine green beans, chopped
¾ pint (450 ml) water
1 bay leaf
1 oz (30 g) plain white flour
1 pint (600 ml) skimmed milk
4 oz (120 g) Cheddar cheese, grated
salt and freshly ground black pepper
chopped fresh parsley, to garnish

1. Melt the margarine in a saucepan and gently cook the onion, potatoes, leek, carrots and beans for 5 minutes. Add the water and bay leaf, bring to the boil and simmer for 15–20 minutes or until the vegetables are tender.
2. Mix the flour with a little of the milk, and gradually mix in the remainder of the milk. Pour the milk mixture into the soup and stir until it thickens. Simmer gently for 5 minutes. Remove the pan from the heat and stir in the cheese, reserving a little to sprinkle over the soup before serving. Season to taste.
3. Ladle the soup into four warmed serving bowls and sprinkle over the remaining cheese. Serve immediately, garnished with the parsley.

Selections per serving:
½ Carbohydrate; ½ Fat; ½ Milk; 1 Protein; 1¼ Vegetable;
20 Optional Calories

Orange and Lentil Soup

Serves 4

Preparation time: 5 minutes
Cooking time: 35 minutes
Calories per serving: 265

Freezing recommended

V **If using vegetarian margarine**

2 teaspoons sunflower
  margarine
1 onion, chopped roughly
1 celery stick, chopped
8 oz (240 g) carrots, diced
8 oz (240 g) peeled celeriac, diced

4 oz (120 g) red lentils, rinsed
1/2 teaspoon dried thyme
1 1/2 pints (900 ml) vegetable
  stock
4 fl oz (120 ml) orange juice
zest of 1 orange
1 bay leaf
salt and freshly ground black
  pepper
5 fl oz (150 ml) low-fat natural
  yogurt, to serve
4 × 1 oz (30 g) slices of
  wholemeal crusty bread,
  to serve

1. Melt the margarine in a large saucepan and cook the onion, celery, carrots and celeriac for 8–10 minutes until softened. Add the remaining ingredients (except the yogurt) and bring to the boil, then reduce the heat and simmer, covered, for 20 minutes.
2. Allow the soup to cool slightly, then purée it in batches in a blender or food processor, adding a little water if the soup is very thick. Return the puréed soup to the saucepan and reheat gently.
3. Season to taste and ladle the soup into warmed serving bowls. Swirl in the yogurt and serve immediately, accompanied by the bread.

Selections per serving:
1 Carbohydrate; 1/2 Fat; 1/4 Milk; 1 Protein; 1 3/4 Vegetable;
15 Optional Calories

Potato and Broccoli Soup

Serves 4

Preparation time: 10 minutes
Cooking time: 40 minutes
Calories per serving: 230

Freezing recommended

V **If using vegetarian margarine**

2 teaspoons sunflower
  margarine
1 onion, chopped roughly
1 garlic clove, crushed

12 oz (360 g) potatoes, peeled
  and diced
1 lb (480 g) broccoli, broken
  into small florets
1 1/2 pints (900 ml) vegetable
  stock
1/2 pint (300 ml) skimmed milk
a pinch of nutmeg
salt and freshly ground black
  pepper
1 oz (30 g) toasted flaked
  almonds, to serve

1. Melt the margarine in a saucepan and gently cook the onion, garlic and potatoes, covered, for 10 minutes. Add the broccoli and stock and bring to the boil, then reduce the heat, cover the pan and simmer for 20–25 minutes.
2. Remove the pan from the heat and stir in the milk. Purée the soup in batches in a food processor or blender and return it to the pan.
3. Add the nutmeg and seasoning to taste, and reheat the soup. Ladle the soup into four warmed serving bowls and scatter over the toasted almonds. Serve immediately.

Selections per serving:
1/2 Carbohydrate; 1 Fat; 1/4 Milk; 1 1/4 Vegetable; 35 Optional Calories

Eggs

I have devoted an entire chapter to eggs because of their immense versatility within the Weight Watchers Programme. ⊗ This chapter is full of exciting dishes including Italian-Style Stuffed Pancakes, a delicious New Potato, Spinach and Feta Frittata, and a very simple and extremely appetising Cheese and Mustard Bread Pudding.

New Potato, Spinach and Feta Frittata

Serves 4

Preparation time: 5 minutes
Cooking time: 20 minutes
Calories per serving: 300

Freezing not recommended

V If using free-range eggs

This Italian-style omelette is very quick and easy, and makes a really tasty, satisfying meal. I like to serve it simply accompanied by a fresh crisp salad.

4 teaspoons sunflower oil
1 onion, chopped
1 garlic clove, crushed (optional)
12 oz (360 g) small new potatoes, cooked and quartered lengthways
4 oz (120 g) frozen spinach, thawed and squeezed
a pinch of freshly grated nutmeg
5 eggs, beaten
4 oz (120 g) feta or Wensleydale cheese, crumbled
salt and freshly ground black pepper

1. Heat the oil in a large frying-pan and cook the onion and garlic (if used), for about 5 minutes until softened. Add the cooked potatoes and stir-fry for 5 minutes. Then stir in the spinach and lower the heat.
2. Add the seasoning and nutmeg to the eggs and pour them into the pan. Tilt the pan, allowing the egg to flow around the vegetables. Cook gently for about 5 minutes until all the egg is almost set. Remove the pan from the heat. Preheat the grill.
3. Sprinkle over the feta or Wensleydale cheese and place the pan under the grill for 2 minutes. Serve immediately, cut into wedges.

Cook's note:
It is important that the spinach is thoroughly squeezed to extract all the excess moisture before using. I find that the easiest way to do this is to place it in a metal sieve and rub the spinach with a spoon.

Selections per serving:
1/2 Carbohydrate; 1 Fat; 2 Protein; 3/4 Vegetable; 35 Optional Calories

Cheese and Mustard Bread Pudding

Serves 4

Preparation time: 10 minutes
Cooking time: 25 minutes
Calories per serving: 430

Freezing not recommended

V If using vegetarian margarine and cheese and free-range eggs

8 × 1 oz (30 g) slices wholemeal bread

4 teaspoons sunflower margarine
English mustard, for spreading
4 oz (120 g) mature Cheddar cheese, grated
1/2 teaspoon oil, for greasing
1 pint (600 ml) skimmed milk
4 eggs, beaten
2 tablespoons chopped fresh parsley
salt and freshly ground black pepper

1. Preheat the oven to Gas Mark 5/190°C/375°F.
2. Spread the bread with the margarine and mustard to taste. Make four rounds of sandwiches with the grated cheese and then cut each sandwich into halves or quarters.
3. Overlap the sandwiches in a greased, shallow ovenproof dish, packing them in tightly.
4. Beat the milk, eggs, parsley and seasoning together and pour the egg mixture over the sandwiches. Bake the pudding for 20–25 minutes or until the egg mixture is just set and the top is lightly browned. Serve immediately.

Selections per serving:
2 Carbohydrate; 1 Fat; 1/2 Milk; 2 Protein; 5 Optional Calories

Italian-style Stuffed Pancakes

Serves 4

Preparation time: making sauce + 15 minutes
Cooking time: 1 hour
Calories per serving: 415

Freezing recommended

V If using free-range eggs

This recipe looks lengthy but I always make up the pancakes and sauce in advance and simply assemble the dish in the evening. It is well worth the effort.

For the pancakes:
4 oz (120 g) plain flour
a pinch of salt
1 egg
½ pint (300 ml) skimmed milk
2 teaspoons vegetable oil

For the filling:
1 teaspoon vegetable oil
1 onion, chopped
2 garlic cloves, crushed
1 small leek, chopped
8 oz (240 g) frozen spinach, thawed and squeezed
8 oz (240 g) cooked peeled potato, diced
8 oz (240 g) ricotta cheese
a pinch of freshly grated nutmeg
salt and freshly ground black pepper

For the topping:
1 quantity (to serve 4) Creamy Tomato Sauce (page 72)
1 oz (30 g) Cheddar cheese, grated finely

1. To make the pancakes, sift the flour and salt into a bowl and make a well in the centre. Break the egg into the well and beat it with a wooden spoon, then gradually beat in the milk, drawing the flour in from the sides to make a smooth batter.

2. Heat a 7-inch (18 cm) non-stick frying-pan. Dip a piece of kitchen paper in the oil and wipe it round the pan in order to grease it lightly. Pour in just enough batter to coat the base of the pan thinly. Cook for 1–2 minutes until golden brown. Turn or toss the pancake over and cook the second side until golden. Transfer the pancake to a plate and repeat the process with the remaining batter, greasing the pan each time, to make eight pancakes. Stack them, interleaved with baking parchment or kitchen paper as you go.

3. To make the filling, heat the oil in a frying-pan and gently cook the onion, garlic and leek, covered, until softened. Stir in the spinach and cook for a further minute. Remove the pan from the heat and stir in the potato, ricotta cheese, nutmeg and seasoning to taste.

4. Preheat the oven to Gas Mark 6/200°C/400°F. Lay out the pancakes and divide the filling equally between them, spooning it across one end of each pancake. Roll up the pancakes and arrange them, seam-side down, in a shallow ovenproof dish. Pour over the tomato sauce and sprinkle over the Cheddar cheese.

5. Bake the pancakes for 30 minutes or until the topping bubbles. Serve immediately, accompanied by assorted steamed vegetables or a crisp green salad.

Cook's note:
Alternatively, the pancake batter ingredients can be mixed together in a food processor or blender. Put the egg and liquid in first, then add the flour and process until smooth.

Selections per serving:
1½ Carbohydrate; ½ Fat; ¼ Milk; 1½ Protein; 4 Vegetable; 30 Optional Calories

Cheesy Souffléd Tuna-stuffed Tomatoes

Serves 4

Preparation time: 10 minutes
Cooking time: 35 minutes
Calories per serving: 285

Freezing not recommended

8 extra-large tomatoes
8 oz (240 g) canned tuna in brine, drained
1 onion, chopped finely
1 red pepper, de-seeded and diced
2 eggs, separated
2 oz (60 g) fresh white breadcrumbs
1 tablespoon chopped fresh basil
2 oz (60 g) Cheddar cheese, grated finely
salt and freshly ground black pepper
fresh basil leaves, to garnish

1. Slice the tops off the tomatoes, scoop out the centres and discard them. Turn the tomatoes upside down on a plate to drain.
2. Meanwhile, mix together the tuna, onion, pepper, egg yolks, breadcrumbs, basil and seasoning. In a separate bowl, whisk the egg whites until stiff and fold them very gently into the tuna mixture.
3. Preheat the oven to Gas Mark 5/190°C/375°F. Spoon the filling into the tomato shells and arrange them tightly in a shallow, non-stick ovenproof dish. Sprinkle over the cheese and bake the tomatoes for 25–30 minutes or until the filling is firm. Serve immediately, garnished with fresh basil leaves.

Selections per serving:
1/2 Carbohydrate; 2 Protein; 4 1/2 Vegetable

Creamy Baked Root Vegetables

Serves 4

Preparation time: 15 minutes
Cooking time: 20 minutes
Calories per serving: 305

Freezing not recommended

V If using free-range eggs and vegetarian Cheddar cheese

I have a real weakness for dauphinoise potatoes baked with cheese and double cream! This dish is a superb alternative which helped me while I was following the Weight Watchers Programme. It makes a wonderful supper when served with assorted steamed vegetables.

8 oz (240 g) parsnips, peeled and cut into 2-inch (5 cm) matchsticks
8 oz (240 g) swede, peeled and cut into 2-inch (5 cm) matchsticks
8 oz (240 g) potatoes, peeled and cut into 2-inch (5 cm) matchsticks
12 oz (360 g) low-fat (up to 8%) fromage frais
2 eggs, beaten
2 oz (60 g) Cheddar cheese, grated
salt and freshly ground black pepper

1. Blanch the root vegetables in boiling water for 1 minute or until tender to the bite. Drain them well and tip them into an ovenproof dish.
2. Preheat the oven to Gas Mark 6/200°C/400°F. Whisk the fromage frais, eggs and seasoning together and spoon the mixture over the vegetables. Sprinkle with the Cheddar cheese and bake the dish for 20 minutes, until golden brown and bubbling.

Selections per serving:
1 Carbohydrate; 2 1/2 Protein; 3/4 Vegetable

Haddock, Egg and Cheese Baked Potatoes

Serves 4

Preparation time: 10 minutes
Cooking time: 1 hour
Calories per serving: 320

Freezing not recommended

4 × 8 oz (240 g) baking
potatoes, scrubbed and
pricked
8 oz (240 g) skinless smoked
haddock fillet
1/2 small onion, chopped very
finely

1 tablespoon freshly squeezed
lemon juice
1/4 pint (150 ml) skimmed milk
4 teaspoons low-fat spread
2 eggs, hard-boiled and
chopped
2 tablespoons chopped fresh
chives
2 oz (60 g) mature Cheddar
cheese, grated
salt and freshly ground black
pepper

1. Preheat the oven to Gas Mark 7/220°C/425°F. Bake the potatoes for about 1 hour, until tender.
2. Meanwhile, place the haddock and onion in a small saucepan and pour over the lemon juice and milk. Slowly bring to the boil, cover the pan and simmer for about 5 minutes or until the fish flakes. Transfer the fish from the pan, with a fish slice, to a plate. Reserve the milk. Flake the fish.
3. Cut the baked potatoes in half and scoop out the flesh into a bowl. Add the low-fat spread, reserved cooking liquid and seasoning and mash until smooth.
4. Stir in the flaked fish, chopped egg and chives and pile the mixture into the potato shells. Serve immediately, sprinkled with the cheese.

Cook's note:
You can place the stuffed potatoes briefly under a grill before serving, to melt the cheese.

Selections per serving:
2 Carbohydrate; 1/2 Fat; 1 1/2 Protein; 1/4 Vegetable; 25 Optional Calories

Pies, Pizzas and Flans

If you are a lover of pastry or pizzas, they are a temptation that is hard to resist, and the commercial varieties are invariably packed with Calories. 🕐 I have therefore created an array of mouth-watering pastry flans, parcels, pies and pizzas which are full of flavour rather than Calories, and fit in with the Weight Watchers Programme so that you don't feel deprived. 🕐 The tempting recipes include impressive Salmon Parcels made with filo pastry, a traditional Steak and Kidney Pie and a Speedy Tomato, Bacon and Mozzarella Bread-stick Pizza.

Speedy Tomato, Bacon and Mozzarella Bread-stick Pizza

Serves 4

Preparation time: 5 minutes
Cooking time: 10 minutes
Calories per serving: 290

Freezing not recommended

Bread-stick pizzas really helped me while I was following the Weight Watchers Programme as they make quick, tasty snacks – ideal for emergencies when those hunger pangs are getting out of control!

2 × 4 oz (120 g) small baguettes, halved lengthways

For the tomato sauce:
6 tablespoons passata (sieved tomatoes)
1 garlic clove, crushed
1 tablespoon tomato purée
a pinch of mixed dried herbs
For the topping:
2 oz (60 g) lean back bacon, grilled and chopped
2 tomatoes, sliced
1 small green pepper, de-seeded and chopped
1/4 onion, sliced
4 closed-cup mushrooms, sliced
4 oz (120 g) mozzarella cheese, sliced thinly

1. Preheat the grill. Toast the cut side of the baguettes until golden. Keep the grill at a medium heat.
2. Mix together all the ingredients for the tomato sauce and spread the sauce over the toasted side of the baguettes.
3. Arrange the topping ingredients over the pizzas, finishing with the mozzarella cheese. Place the pizzas under the grill for 5 minutes or until they are heated through and the cheese is melted. Serve immediately.

Selections per serving:
2 Carbohydrate; 2 Protein; 1¼ Vegetable

Tasty Tuna and Prawn Pizza

Serves 4

Preparation time: 10 minutes
Cooking time: 20 minutes
Calories per serving: 410

Freezing not recommended

For the base:
6 oz (180 g) self-raising flour
a pinch of salt
8 teaspoons sunflower margarine
4 fl oz (120 ml) skimmed milk
1 tablespoon flour, for rolling
For the tomato sauce:
1/4 pint (150 ml) passata
2 garlic cloves, crushed

2 tablespoons tomato purée
a pinch of mixed dried herbs
For the topping:
1/2 onion, cut into thin wedges
1 courgette, sliced
4 oz (120 g) canned tuna in brine, drained and flaked
2 oz (60 g) cooked peeled prawns
4 oz (120 g) button mushrooms, sliced
1 tablespoon capers
3 oz (90 g) Cheddar cheese, grated

1. To make the base, sift together the flour and salt and rub in the margarine. Then stir in enough of the milk to give a soft but not sticky dough.
2. Roll the dough out on a lightly floured surface to a 12-inch (30 cm) round, and place it on a baking sheet lined with baking parchment.
3. Mix together the passata, garlic and tomato purée. Spread the sauce over the base and sprinkle with the dried herbs.
4. Preheat the oven to Gas Mark 6/200°C/400°F. Arrange the topping ingredients over the pizza, finishing with the cheese.
5. Bake the pizza for 15–20 minutes or until golden and bubbling. Serve hot or cold.

Selections per serving:
1½ Carbohydrate; 2 Fat; 1½ Protein; 1 Vegetable; 20 Optional Calories

Steak and Kidney Pie

Serves 4

Preparation time: 20 minutes
+ 30 minutes chilling
Cooking time: 2 hours
35 minutes
Calories per serving: 295

Freezing recommended

6 oz (180 g) trimmed braising
  steak
2 oz (60 g) ox kidney, cored
1 tablespoon seasoned flour
1 onion, chopped
2 carrots, chopped
4 oz (120 g) swede, peeled and
  diced

3/4 pint (450 ml) beef stock
1 bay leaf
a sprig of fresh thyme or 1/2
  teaspoon dried thyme
1 tablespoon Worcestershire
  sauce
1 tablespoon tomato purée
6 oz (180 g) button mushrooms
6 oz (180 g) puff pastry, thawed
  if frozen
1 tablespoon skimmed milk
salt and freshly ground black
  pepper

1. Place the braising steak on the rack of the grill pan and grill, turning once, until the fat stops dripping. Dice the steak and kidneys, and coat them with the seasoned flour. Put the meat in a large saucepan with the onion, carrots, swede, stock, bay leaf, thyme, Worcestershire sauce and tomato purée.
2. Bring the contents of the pan to the boil, then reduce the heat, cover and simmer, stirring frequently, for 2 hours or until the meat is tender. If the mixture becomes dry, simply add a little water. Season with salt and pepper and mix in the mushrooms. Spoon the meat and vegetables into a pie dish and chill for 20–30 minutes in the refrigerator.
3. Preheat the oven to Gas Mark 6/200°C/400°F. Roll out the pastry 1 inch (2.5 cm) larger than the top of the dish. Cut a 1/2-inch (1 cm) strip from around the edge of the pastry and place this strip around the rim of the dish. Dampen the edges of the pastry lid with water and place the pastry on top of the dish, pressing down the edges to seal.
4. Brush the top with the milk and bake the pie for 20–30 minutes or until puffed up and golden.

Selections per serving:
1 Protein; 1 1/2 Vegetable; 195 Optional Calories

Open-crust Chicken and Mushroom Pie

Serves 6

Preparation time: 20 minutes
+ 30 minutes chilling
Cooking time: 55 minutes
Calories per serving: 265

Freezing not recommended

Do not worry if the pastry breaks while you are assembling the pie – simply patch it up, as this gives the pie its rustic character.

For the pastry:
4 oz (120 g) plain flour
a pinch of salt
2 oz (60 g) block margarine
3–4 tablespoons ice-cold water
2 tablespoons plain flour, for
  rolling

For the filling:
1 teaspoon sunflower oil
6 oz (180 g) skinless, boneless
  chicken breast, diced
1 onion, chopped
1 garlic clove, crushed
  (optional)
4 oz (120 g) closed-cup
  mushrooms, sliced
8 tomatoes, peeled and
  chopped
2 tablespoons tomato purée
1 large courgette, chopped
1 tablespoon chopped fresh
  tarragon or 1 teaspoon dried
  tarragon
1 egg, separated
1 tablespoon semolina
1 teaspoon grated parmesan
  cheese
salt and freshly ground black
  pepper

1. To make the pastry, sift the flour and salt into a large bowl, then lightly rub in the fat until it resembles fine breadcrumbs. Stir in enough ice-cold water, using a blunt-ended knife, to form a soft but not sticky dough. Knead the dough lightly until smooth, then place it in a polythene bag and chill for 30 minutes in the refrigerator.
2. To make the filling, heat the oil in a non-stick frying-pan and cook the chicken, onion and garlic (if used) for 5 minutes over a medium heat. Add the mushrooms, tomatoes, tomato purée, courgette, tarragon and seasoning, and gently simmer for 15 minutes.
3. Roll out the chilled pastry on a lightly floured surface to form a rough 10-inch (25 cm) round and place it on a floured baking sheet.
4. Brush the pastry with egg yolk and sprinkle over the semolina. Spoon over the filling, leaving a 1 1/2-inch (4 cm) border.
5. Preheat the oven to Gas Mark 6/200°C/400°F. Turn the edges of the pastry in to cover part of the filling.
6. Brush the pastry with the egg white and sprinkle over the parmesan. Bake the pie for 30–35 minutes, until golden.

Selections per serving:
1/2 Carbohydrate; 2 Fat; 1/2 Protein; 1 1/2 Vegetable; 55 Optional Calories

Cheese, Leek, Tomato and Basil Flan

Serves 6

Preparation and cooking time:
55 minutes + 45 minutes
chilling
Calories per serving: 260

Freezing recommended

V If using free-range eggs,
vegetarian margarine and
Cheddar cheese

For the pastry:
4 oz (120 g) plain flour
a pinch of salt
2 oz (60 g) block margarine
3–4 tablespoons ice-cold water

2 tablespoons flour, for rolling
For the filling:
4 oz (120 g) half-fat soft cheese
    with garlic and herbs
2 eggs, beaten
1 tablespoon chopped fresh
    basil
1 leek, sliced thinly and cooked
3 tomatoes, peeled, de-seeded
    and chopped
1 oz (30 g) Cheddar cheese,
    grated
salt and freshly ground black
    pepper
fresh basil leaves, to garnish

1. To make the pastry, sift the flour and salt into a bowl and rub in the margarine, using your fingertips, until the mixture resembles fine breadcrumbs. With a blunt-ended knife, stir in enough water to form a soft but not sticky dough. Knead the dough gently until smooth, then wrap it in a polythene bag or aluminium foil and chill it for 30 minutes in the refrigerator.
2. Preheat the oven to Gas Mark 6/200°C/400°F. Roll out the chilled pastry on a lightly floured surface and use it to line an 8-inch (20 cm) sandwich cake tin. Chill for 10–15 minutes, then prick the base with a fork and line the case with aluminium foil, or baking parchment and baking beans.
3. Bake the pastry case blind for 5 minutes or until the pastry is just set. Lift out the foil or baking parchment and beans and bake for a further 5 minutes or until the base is just firm. Turn the oven down to Gas Mark 5/190°C/375°F.
4. To make the filling, beat the soft cheese until smooth. Gradually beat in the eggs, and then stir in the basil and seasoning.
5. Arrange the cooked leek and the tomatoes in the base of the pastry case. Sprinkle over the Cheddar cheese, and pour over the egg mixture.
6. Place the flan on a baking sheet and bake for 25–35 minutes or until just set. Serve hot or cold, garnished with fresh basil leaves.

Selections per serving:
1/2 Carbohydrate; 2 Fat; 1 Protein; 3/4 Vegetable; 35 Optional Calories

Salmon Parcels

Serves 4

Preparation time: 15 minutes
Cooking time: 15 minutes
Calories per serving: 200

Freezing not recommended

These quick and easy salmon parcels look really impressive, making them ideal for a special occasion. I like to serve them with Baked Chips (page 34) and steamed broccoli florets.

2 oz (60 g) Total light greek
    yogurt
1 tablespoon chopped fresh dill
    or 1 teaspoon dried dill
1/2 teaspoon lemon juice
4 × 3 oz (90 g) pieces salmon
    fillet, skinned
8 teaspoons low-fat spread
8 × 7-inch (18 cm) square filo
    pastry sheets, thawed if
    frozen
1/4 teaspoon sesame seeds
sprigs of fresh dill, to garnish

1. Mix the yogurt with the dill and lemon juice, and spread the mixture over the tops of the salmon fillets.
2. Melt the low-fat spread in a small saucepan and lightly brush it over four of the filo pastry squares. Cover with the remaining filo sheets and brush the tops with a little more of the low-fat spread.
3. Preheat the oven to Gas Mark 6/200°C/400°F. Place a salmon fillet in the centre of each pastry layer. Fold over the sides, and then roll up the salmon in the pastry to form a small enclosed parcel. Use the remaining melted low-fat spread to grease a baking sheet and to brush over the top of the parcels.
4. Place the parcels on the baking sheet, seam-side down, and sprinkle over the sesame seeds. Bake for about 15 minutes or until golden brown. Serve immediately, garnished with sprigs of fresh dill.

Cook's note:
Keep the filo pastry covered whilst not in use or it will dry out and crack. I have used Total light greek yogurt which is now available from major supermarkets and has a wonderful creamy taste.

Selections per serving:
1/2 Carbohydrate; 1 Fat; 2 Protein; 10 Optional Calories

One-pot Meals and Bakes

All the meals in this chapter are designed to be made in one pot or dish and simmered or baked to perfection. ⊗ Recipes include meat, fish, beans or lentils and a selection of vegetables which are combined with various aromatic spices and fragrant herbs to create a wide variety of dishes including stews, curries, potato-topped bakes, moussakas and stuffed vegetables.

I have also included Baked Chips, which are bound to be a real winner with all the family. ⊗ They require very little fat, so they fit easily into the Programme and taste better than any deep-fried chip – who says that you can't eat chips and lose weight?

Baked Fish Parcels

Serves 4

Preparation time: 10 minutes
Cooking time: 10 minutes
Calories per serving: 130

Freezing not recommended

4 × 4 oz (120 g) cod or halibut
  steaks
2 teaspoons margarine
2 garlic cloves, crushed
2 shallots, chopped very finely
4 tomatoes, peeled, de-seeded
  and chopped
2 tablespoons freshly squeezed
  lemon juice
2 tablespoons dry white wine
1 tablespoon chopped fresh
  parsley
salt and freshly ground black
  pepper

1. Cut out four large pieces of baking parchment or aluminium foil and place a fish steak in the centre of each.
2. Mix together the margarine and garlic and dot this over the fish.
3. In a small bowl, mix together the shallots, tomatoes and lemon juice and spoon the mixture evenly over the fish. Drizzle over the wine, and sprinkle the steaks with the parsley and seasoning.
4. Preheat the oven to Gas Mark 6/200°C/400°F. Gather the edges of the baking parchment or aluminium foil together to form a parcel, and fold them over to seal. Place the parcels on a baking sheet and bake for 10 minutes or until the fish is cooked through. Serve the parcels unopened so that the aroma can be appreciated at the table.

Selections per serving:
1/2 Fat; 2 Protein; 3/4 Vegetable; 10 Optional Calories

Baked Fish Cakes

Serves 4

Preparation time: 10 minutes
Cooking time: 50 minutes
Calories per serving: 340

Freezing recommended

12 oz (360 g) peeled potatoes,
  chopped
2 teaspoons margarine
2 oz (60 g) Cheddar cheese,
  grated
12 oz (360 g) cooked firm white
  fish or canned tuna in brine,
  drained and flaked
1/2 small onion, chopped very
  finely
1 egg, beaten
3 oz (90 g) fresh white or
  wholemeal breadcrumbs
salt and freshly ground black
  pepper

1. Cook the potatoes in plenty of boiling salted water until tender. Drain the potatoes well, then return them to the saucepan and mash them with the margarine until smooth. Stir in the cheese and then add the remaining ingredients except the egg and breadcrumbs, and mix thoroughly. Season to taste and allow to cool.
2. Divide the mixture into eight and shape them into flat rounds. Dip them in the beaten egg and drain them thoroughly before coating them with the breadcrumbs.
3. Preheat the oven to Gas Mark 5/190°C/375°F. Place the fish cakes on a baking sheet lined with baking parchment and bake for 30 minutes or until golden. Serve immediately.

Selections per serving:
1 1/2 Carbohydrate; 1/2 Fat; 2 Protein; 15 Optional Calories

Creamy Haddock and Prawn Potato Bake

Serves 4

Preparation time: 15 minutes
Cooking time: 50 minutes
Calories per serving: 450

Freezing recommended

This dish contains potatoes and a variety of vegetables, making it a really satisfying meal in itself.

3/4 pint (450 ml) skimmed milk
4 peppercorns
1 bay leaf
4 oz (120 g) skinless haddock fillet
4 oz (120 g) skinless smoked haddock fillet
4 teaspoons low-fat spread
2 onions, chopped
1 leek, sliced thinly
2 carrots, chopped
4 oz (120 g) small broccoli florets
1 courgette, sliced
2 oz (60 g) frozen peas
1 oz (30 g) plain flour
4 tablespoons single cream
4 oz (120 g) large peeled prawns, thawed if frozen
2 teaspoons chopped fresh dill or 1 teaspoon dried dill
1 1/2 lb (720 g) potatoes, peeled, parboiled and sliced thinly
2 oz (60 g) Cheddar cheese, grated
salt and freshly ground black pepper

1. Pour the milk into a small saucepan and add the peppercorns, bay leaf and fish. Slowly bring to the boil, then cover the pan and simmer for 8 minutes or until the fish flakes. Using a fish slice, transfer the fish to a plate and flake it. Strain the milk and reserve it.
2. Melt the low-fat spread in a saucepan and gently cook the onions for 3–4 minutes, then stir in the leek, carrots, broccoli and courgette, and continue to cook for 5 minutes.
3. Stir in the peas and then the flour, and cook for 1 minute. Gradually add the reserved milk, stirring continuously until the sauce thickens. Remove the pan from the heat and fold in the poached fish, cream, prawns, dill and seasoning.
4. Preheat the oven to Gas Mark 6/200°C/400°F. Spoon the mixture into an ovenproof dish and overlap the potato slices on top. Sprinkle over the cheese and bake the dish for 20–25 minutes until golden. Serve immediately.

Selections per serving:
1 1/2 Carbohydrate; 1/2 Fat; 1/4 Milk; 1 1/2 Protein; 2 Vegetable; 110 Optional Calories

Fragrant Chicken, Spinach and Tomato Curry

Serves 4

Preparation time: 10 minutes
Cooking time: 50 minutes
Calories per serving: 440

Freezing recommended

4 teaspoons sunflower oil
2 onions, chopped finely
2 garlic cloves, crushed
8 oz (240 g) potatoes, peeled and diced
6 oz (180 g) skinless, boneless chicken breast, diced
1 tablespoon grated fresh root ginger
1 tablespoon garam masala
4 cardamom pods, crushed
2 oz (60 g) red lentils
3/4 pt (450 ml) water
4 tomatoes, peeled, de-seeded and chopped
4 oz (120 g) frozen chopped spinach leaves
4 oz (120 g) small cauliflower florets
2 tablespoons chopped fresh coriander or 2 teaspoons dried coriander
salt and freshly ground black pepper
chopped fresh coriander, plus a few sprigs to garnish
1 1/2 lb (720 g) freshly cooked basmati rice, to serve

1. Heat the oil in a large pan and gently cook the onion, garlic and potatoes until golden. Stir in the chicken, ginger, garam masala and cardamom pods, and stir-fry until the chicken is sealed.
2. Stir in the lentils and water. Bring to the boil, then reduce the heat and simmer for 15 minutes. Stir in the tomatoes, spinach, cauliflower and 2 tablespoons of fresh coriander (or 2 teaspoons of dried coriander), cover the pan and simmer for a further 20 minutes or until the vegetables and lentils are tender. Stir frequently to ensure that the mixture does not stick, and add a little water if it becomes very thick.
3. Season to taste and serve immediately, garnished with the coriander and accompanied by the freshly cooked rice.

Selections per serving:
2 1/2 Carbohydrate; 1 Fat; 1 1/2 Protein; 2 Vegetable

(𝒱) **Vegetarian option:**
Replace the chicken with 8 oz (240 g) Quorn chunks, adding them with the lentils. This will not affect the total Selections or Calories per serving.

Baked Chips

Serves 4

Preparation time: 10 minutes
Cooking time: 30 minutes
Calories per serving: 215

Freezing not recommended

V

These are a real discovery which you are guaranteed to be hooked on for life. They are the dieter's dream which a friend of mine revealed to me – low-fat chips that taste even better than deep-fried chips! You have to try them to believe them. Even Andy, my husband, who is a fried-food worshipper, is hooked!

2 lb (960 g) Maris Piper potatoes, peeled and cut into strips
4 teaspoons vegetable oil

1. Dry the potatoes thoroughly with kitchen paper and place them in a large plastic box. Pour in the oil, put a lid on the box and shake the box vigorously to coat the chips.
2. Preheat the oven to Gas Mark 7/220°C/425°F. Spread the chips on a baking sheet lined with baking parchment and bake for 25–30 minutes until golden and crisp. Serve immediately.

Selections per serving:
2 Carbohydrate; 1 Fat

Stuffed Baked Peppers

Serves 4

Preparation time: 10 minutes
Cooking time: 1 hour
10 minutes
Calories per serving: 275

Freezing recommended

V If using vegetarian margarine and Cheddar cheese

4 equal-sized red peppers, halved lengthways and de-seeded
2 teaspoons sunflower margarine
1 onion, chopped
2 garlic cloves, crushed
1 courgette, chopped
3 oz (90 g) button mushrooms, sliced
14 oz (420 g) canned chopped tomatoes
1 tablespoon tomato purée
3 oz (90 g) brown rice
1/4 pint (150 ml) vegetable stock
2 teaspoons fresh thyme leaves or 1 teaspoon dried thyme
2 oz (60 g) mature Cheddar cheese, grated finely
1 oz (30 g) fresh white breadcrumbs
salt and freshly ground black pepper
1/2 teaspoon oil, for greasing

1. Blanch the pepper shells in salted boiling water for 2–3 minutes and drain well.
2. Heat the margarine in a large saucepan and cook the onion and garlic for 5 minutes or until softened. Add the courgette and mushrooms and cook for 3 minutes.
3. Stir in the tomatoes, tomato purée, rice, stock and thyme. Bring to the boil, then reduce the heat, cover the pan and simmer, stirring frequently, for 30 minutes or until the rice is tender and the mixture is thick. Remove the pan from the heat and season to taste. If the mixture becomes dry before the rice is cooked, simply add some water to the pan.
4. Preheat the oven to Gas Mark 6/200°C/400°F. Place the pepper shells in a greased, shallow ovenproof dish and spoon in the rice mixture. Sprinkle over the cheese and then the breadcrumbs.
5. Bake for 15–20 minutes and serve immediately.

Selections per serving:
1 Carbohydrate; 1/2 Fat; 1/2 Protein; 33/4 Vegetable; 5 Optional Calories

Pork, Prune and Apple Stew

Serves 4

Preparation time: 10 minutes
Cooking time: 1 hour
10 minutes
Calories per serving: 385

Freezing recommended

12 oz (360 g) lean pork, cubed
8 teaspoons sunflower oil
1 large onion, chopped
1 garlic clove, crushed
1 oz (30 g) plain flour
2 teaspoons paprika

1 teaspoon mustard powder
2 celery sticks, sliced diagonally
2 carrots, sliced diagonally
8 fl oz (240 ml) dry cider
8 fl oz (240 ml) vegetable stock
12 oz (360 g) cooking apples,
    peeled and sliced
3 oz (90 g) pitted ready-to-eat
    prunes, quartered
salt and freshly ground black
    pepper
1½ lb (720 g) freshly cooked
    long-grain rice, to serve

1. Place the pork on the rack of the grill pan and grill, turning once, until the fat stops dripping.
2. Heat the oil in a large pan and cook the onion and garlic until softened. Add the pork, flour, paprika and mustard powder, and cook for 1 minute, stirring.
3. Add the celery and carrots to the pan and then gradually stir in the cider and stock. Bring to the boil, stirring, until thickened and smooth. Reduce the heat, cover the pan and simmer for 30 minutes.
4. Add the apple slices, prunes and seasoning, stir well and continue to simmer for 20–30 minutes or until the pork is cooked through. Serve immediately with the freshly cooked rice.

Selections per serving:
2 Carbohydrate; 2 Fat; 1½ Fruit; 2 Protein; 1 Vegetable;
55 Optional Calories

Beef and Horseradish Cottage Pie

Serves 4

Preparation time: 10 minutes
Cooking time: 45 minutes
Calories per serving: 400

Freezing recommended

2 teaspoons sunflower oil
2 onions, chopped
2–3 garlic cloves, crushed
1 red pepper, de-seeded and
    chopped
1 green pepper, de-seeded and
    chopped
8 oz (240 g) extra-lean minced
    beef
6 oz (180 g) canned cannellini
    or kidney beans, rinsed and
    drained

2 tablespoons tomato purée
2 × 14 oz (420 g) canned
    chopped tomatoes
¼ pint (150 ml) vegetable stock
1 bay leaf
2 oz (60 g) closed-cup chestnut
    mushrooms, sliced
1 tablespoon chopped fresh
    parsley
salt and freshly ground black
    pepper
For the topping:
2 lb (960 g) potatoes, peeled
    and roughly chopped
4 teaspoons low-fat spread
2 tablespoons English
    horseradish mustard
4 tablespoons skimmed milk

1. Heat the oil in a large saucepan and cook the onions, garlic and peppers until softened. Meanwhile, in a frying pan, cook the minced beef until browned. Pour off any fat. Add the minced beef to the vegetable mixture. Stir in the beans, tomato purée, tomatoes, stock, bay leaf, mushrooms, parsley and seasoning and simmer for 20–25 minutes, partially covered.
2. Meanwhile cook the potatoes in boiling salted water for 20 minutes. Drain the potatoes well, return them to the pan and heat gently to dry them out. Add the low-fat spread, mustard and milk, and mash until smooth. Season to taste.
3. Preheat the oven to Gas Mark 6/200°C/400°F. Remove the bay leaf from the minced beef and spoon the mixture into a deep ovenproof dish. Pile the potato on top. Bake for 15 minutes or until the potato is crispy. Serve immediately.

Selections per serving:
2 Carbohydrate; 1 Fat; 2 Protein; 4 Vegetable; 5 Optional Calories

(𝒱) **Vegetarian option:**
Substitute 8 oz (240 g) Quorn mince for the minced beef and simply add it to the pan with the beans. This will reduce the Protein Selections to 1½ and the total Calories to 355 per serving.

Rich Bean Moussaka
Serves 4

Preparation time: 10 minutes
+ draining
Cooking time: 1 hour
40 minutes
Calories per serving: 505

Freezing recommended

V If using free-range eggs
and vegetarian Cheddar
cheese

This is an adaptation of a
delicious moussaka that I ate
while staying at a farmhouse
in Hereford. It was so
delicious that I made up this
version to fit in with the
Weight Watchers Programme
so as not to miss out! I like to
serve it with a crisp mixed
salad and french bread as the
bake itself does not include
any Carbohydrate Selections.
Remember that 1 oz (30 g)
bread adds 1 Carbohydrate
Selection, and Calories per
serving will increase to 585.

1 large aubergine, sliced
8 teaspoons olive oil
1 large onion, chopped
2 garlic cloves, crushed
1 red pepper, de-seeded and
    chopped
14 oz (420 g) canned chopped
    tomatoes
2 tablespoons tomato purée
9 oz (270 g) canned red kidney
    beans, drained and lightly
    mashed
½ teaspoon ground cinnamon
4 tablespoons red wine
4 tablespoons cornflour
1 pint (600 ml) skimmed milk
4 oz (120 g) mature reduced-fat
    Cheddar cheese
1 egg
salt and freshly ground black
    pepper

1. Place the sliced aubergine in a colander, sprinkle it liberally with
salt and leave it to drain for 30 minutes. Then rinse and dry the
aubergine thoroughly with kitchen paper.
2. Preheat the oven to Gas Mark 5/190°C/375°F. Using 6 teaspoons
of the oil, grease a baking sheet, place the aubergine slices on it in
one layer and brush them with the oil. Bake for 20 minutes or until
golden. Keep the oven at this temperature.
3. Meanwhile heat the remaining oil in a saucepan and cook the
onion, garlic and red pepper for 5 minutes until softened, then add
the tomatoes, tomato purée, beans, cinnamon, wine and seasoning.
Bring to the boil and simmer for 10 minutes.
4. Mix the cornflour with a little of the milk in a saucepan and
then beat in the remaining milk. Cook over a moderate heat,
stirring frequently until thickened. Stir in half the cheese, season to
taste and remove the pan from the heat. Allow the sauce to cool
slightly and beat in the egg.
5. Arrange half of the baked aubergine slices in the base of a
shallow ovenproof dish. Spoon over half of the bean mixture and
half of the white sauce. Repeat the layers, finishing with the white
sauce, and scatter over the remaining cheese.
6. Bake in the oven for about 1 hour, until golden and bubbling.

Cook's note:
This dish tastes even better when warmed up the following day, as
it allows the flavours to develop.

Selections per serving:
2 Fat; ½ Milk; 2 Protein; 4 Vegetable; 40 Optional Calories

Grills and Stir-fries

Grilled meat and stir-fries are really quick to prepare. ✹ This chapter shows you how to jazz up grilled meat and fish with a ginger marinade, minted yogurt coating and a honey and mustard crunchy topping. There is also a fabulous selection of stir-fries which are a great way to make use of any vegetables in the refrigerator and transform them into something special. ✹ Recipes include a Chow Mein Stir-fry incorporating beansprouts, egg-noodles and peanuts, a Chinese Fish Stir-fry with a flavoursome sweet-and-sour spicy sauce, and a Mexican Stir-fry which you wrap up in pancakes at the table.

Grilled Lamb with Minted Yogurt

Serves 4

Preparation time: 5 minutes +
2 hours marinating
Cooking time: 20 minutes
Calories per serving: 380

Freezing not recommended

5 fl oz (150 ml) low-fat thick
    natural yogurt
1–2 garlic cloves, crushed
3 tablespoons chopped fresh
    mint
a pinch of ground cumin
zest of 1/2 lime or lemon
4 × 4 oz (120 g) lean, boneless
    lamb leg steaks
salt and freshly ground black
    pepper
To serve:
4 × 2 oz (60 g) warmed pitta
    breads
mixed salad

1. Mix the yogurt, garlic, mint, cumin and lime or lemon zest together in a dish and season well. Add the lamb and stir to coat, then cover the dish and leave it to marinate for 2 hours.
2. Preheat the grill. Remove the lamb from the yogurt and grill it under a moderate heat for 8–10 minutes. Turn the lamb over, baste it with the yogurt mixture and cook for another 8–10 minutes or until cooked through and golden on each side. Serve immediately with pitta bread and salad.

Cook's note:
Look out for British tenderlean lamb in your local supermarket as it is particularly lean.

Selections per serving:
2 Carbohydrate; 1/4 Milk; 3 Protein

Cod and Prawn Kebabs

Serves 4

Preparation time: 10 minutes
+1 hour marinating
Cooking time: 30 minutes
Calories per serving: 375

Freezing not recommended

For the marinade:
1 onion, grated
2 garlic cloves, crushed
2 teaspoons grated root ginger
1/4 teaspoon chilli powder
3 tablespoons lemon juice
2 tablespoons sunflower oil

For the kebabs:
6 oz (180 g) cooked peeled tiger
    prawns
8 oz (240 g) skinned cod fillet,
    cubed
2 red onions, cut into wedges
1 large courgette, cut into 1/2-
    inch (1 cm) slices
For the spiced rice:
8 oz (240 g) basmati rice
1 pint (600 ml) water
1 cinnamon stick
3 cloves
1 teaspoon turmeric
1 teaspoon cumin seeds
1 oz (30 g) raisins
salt

1. In a bowl, mix together all the marinade ingredients, and stir in the prawns and fish. Cover the bowl with clingfilm and leave to marinate for 1 hour in the refrigerator.
2. Place all the rice ingredients in a saucepan and stir well. Bring to the boil, then simmer, partly covered, for 12–15 minutes or until the rice is tender and has absorbed the water. Turn off the heat and leave the pan to stand, covered. Remove the cloves and cinnamon.
3. Preheat the grill to high. Thread the prawns, fish, onions and courgette on to eight wooden skewers and cook them under the grill for 10–15 minutes, basting them with any remaining marinade, until golden. Serve immediately with the spiced rice.

Selections per serving:
2 Carbohydrate; 1 1/2 Fat; 1 1/2 Protein; 1 Vegetable; 15 Optional Calories

Mexican Stir-fry Pancakes

Serves 4

Preparation time: 10 minutes
Cooking time: 10 minutes
Calories per serving: 505

Freezing not recommended

2 teaspoons sunflower oil
1 large onion, chopped
1 red pepper, de-seeded and
   chopped
1 yellow or orange pepper,
   de-seeded and chopped
1 green pepper, de-seeded and
   chopped
2 courgettes, diced
8 oz (240 g) large prawns

For the tomato relish:
2 extra-large tomatoes, peeled
   and chopped
1 onion, chopped finely
1–2 garlic cloves, crushed
1 small red chilli, de-seeded
   and chopped finely (optional)
a few drops of Tabasco sauce or
   a pinch of Cayenne pepper
For the avocado purée:
1/2 medium-size avocado
1 tablespoon lemon juice
To serve:
4 tablespoons soured cream
8 × 6-inch (15 cm) diameter
   soft flour tortillas

1. In a small serving dish mix together all the ingredients for the tomato relish. Cover the dish and chill in the refrigerator.
2. For the avocado purée blend the avocado and lemon juice in a blender or food processor until smooth. Transfer the purée to a small serving dish, cover it and chill in the refrigerator.
3. Heat the oil in a frying-pan and stir-fry the onion and peppers for about 5 minutes over a high heat until golden. Add the courgettes and prawns and continue to cook until tender.
4. Transfer the stir-fry to a large warmed platter and serve immediately with the bowls of tomato relish, avocado purée, the soured cream and the warmed tortillas. To assemble, spread some soured cream over the tortilla with a spoonful of the tomato relish and avocado purée. Top with a spoonful of the stir-fry, roll up the pancake and eat it with your fingers.

Cook's note:
Smetana is a low-fat soured cream used widely in Eastern European cooking. Wheatflour tortillas are now available from major super-markets. To heat, simply wrap them in aluminium foil and place them in a low oven for a few minutes.

Selections per serving:
2 Carbohydrate; 1 1/2 Fat; 1 Protein; 3 1/2 Vegetable; 50 Optional Calories

(𝒱) **Vegetarian option:**
Simply omit the prawns. Remember that the dish will then have no Protein Selection and the total Calories per serving will be 440.

Grilled Chicken with Spicy Tomato Sauce

Serves 4

Preparation time: 12 minutes
Cooking time: 15 minutes
Calories per serving: 345

Freezing not recommended

12 oz (360 g) skinless, boneless
   chicken breast, cut into large
   chunks
For the sauce:
2 tablespoons olive oil
1 teaspoon ground coriander
1 teaspoon ground cumin
juice of 1 lemon
2 extra-large tomatoes, peeled
   and chopped
1/2 red pepper, de-seeded and
   chopped finely

1 small red chilli, de-seeded
   and chopped finely (optional)
1/2 onion, chopped finely
1–2 tablespoons chopped fresh
   coriander
2 tablespoons tomato purée
salt and freshly ground black
   pepper
To serve:
1/2 medium-size avocado,
   peeled, stoned and sliced
4 tablespoons Total light greek
   yogurt
shredded lettuce
4 × 6-inch (15 cm) diameter
   corn tortillas

1. Mix together all the sauce ingredients except the tomato purée. Spoon 6 tablespoons of the mixture into a separate bowl, cover it with clingfilm and place it in the refrigerator. Mix the tomato purée into the remaining sauce. Add the chicken and stir to coat. Allow the chicken to marinate for 1 hour, or overnight, in the refrigerator.
2. Preheat the grill. Place the marinated chicken in a grill pan, brush over the marinade and cook under the grill for 15 minutes, turning and basting frequently, until the chicken is cooked through.
3. Serve immediately on individual plates with the avocado slices, a spoonful of greek yogurt, some shredded lettuce, the reserved tomato sauce and the tortillas.

Selections per serving:
1 Carbohydrate; 2 1/2 Fat; 2 Protein; 1 1/4 Vegetable; 25 Optional Calories

Chinese Fish Stir-fry

Serves 4

Preparation time: 10 minutes
Cooking time: 5 minutes
Calories per serving: 280

Freezing not recommended

This is a version of a popular dish found in Chinese restaurants which is one of my favourites. It is really flavoursome and simply needs to be served with 3 oz (90 g) plain boiled rice per serving. Remember to add 1 Carbohydrate Selection and 115 Calories per serving.

2 tablespoons groundnut or sunflower oil
2 garlic cloves, diced finely
2-inch (5 cm) piece of ginger, peeled and grated
6 spring onions, shredded
2 carrots, cut into long, thin strips
3 oz (90 g) mange-tout peas
3 oz (90 g) baby sweetcorn, halved lengthways
4 savoy cabbage leaves, shredded
1 red pepper, de-seeded and sliced
7 oz (210 g) canned bamboo shoots, drained
4 oz (120 g) canned water chestnuts, drained
12 oz (360 g) skinless white fish

For the sauce:
6 fl oz (180 ml) unsweetened pineapple juice
2 tablespoons soy sauce
3 tablespoons white wine vinegar
1 teaspoon chilli powder
1/4 pint (150 ml) water
2 tablespoons Sweetex sweetener
2 tablespoons tomato purée
2 tablespoons cornflour

1. Heat the oil in a large frying-pan or wok and stir-fry the garlic, ginger and all the vegetables except for the bamboo shoots and water chestnuts, for 2 minutes.
2. Mix together the sauce ingredients and add them to the pan with the bamboo shoots, water chestnuts and fish. Stir until thickened, then cover the frying-pan or wok and cook for 2 minutes. Serve immediately.

Selections per serving:
1/2 Carbohydrate; 1 1/2 Fat; 1 Protein; 2 1/2 Vegetable; 50 Optional Calories

Chow Mein Stir-fry

Serves 4

Preparation time: 5 minutes
Cooking time: 10 minutes
Calories per serving: 370

Freezing not recommended

V If using wheat noodles

2 tablespoons groundnut or sunflower oil
2 oz (60 g) unsalted peanuts or cashew nuts, chopped
2 garlic cloves, chopped finely
1 leek, halved lengthways and sliced
1 onion, chopped
2 teaspoons freshly grated root ginger
1 fresh red chilli, de-seeded and chopped finely
2 carrots, peeled and sliced diagonally
6 oz (180 g) button mushrooms sliced
2 oz (60 g) fine green beans, halved
6 oz (180 g) thread egg-noodles, cooked according to the directions on the packet, and drained
6 oz (180 g) beansprouts
3 tablespoons light soy sauce
3 tablespoons hoi sin sauce

1. Heat the oil in a wok or large frying-pan and gently cook the chopped nuts until golden. Remove them with a slotted spoon and drain them on kitchen paper.
2. Add the garlic, leek, onion, ginger and chilli to the pan and cook for 2 minutes. Then add the remaining vegetables except the beansprouts and stir-fry for 3–4 minutes.
3. Stir in the noodles, beansprouts, soy sauce and hoi sin sauce, and stir-fry for 1 minute or until hot. Sprinkle over the nuts and serve immediately.

Selections per serving:
1 1/2 Carbohydrate; 2 1/2 Fat; 1/2 Protein; 2 3/4 Vegetable

Crunchy Chicken Stir-fry

Serves 4

Preparation time: 5 minutes
Cooking time: 10 minutes
Calories per serving: 170

Freezing not recommended

1 tablespoon groundnut or
  sunflower oil
8 oz (240 g) skinless, boneless
  chicken breast, cubed
8 spring onions, chopped
1 garlic clove, crushed
1 small red pepper, de-seeded
  and diced
6 oz (180 g) button
  mushrooms, quartered
1 courgette, cut into long, thin
  strips
4 oz (120 g) sugar-snap peas
8 tablespoons yellow bean stir-
  fry sauce

1. Heat the oil in a wok or large frying-pan and stir-fry the chicken for 3–4 minutes until it is cooked through and golden. Remove the chicken from the pan and drain it on kitchen paper.
2. Add all the vegetables to the pan and stir-fry until they are just beginning to soften but still crunchy, and then remove them from the pan.
3. Slowly stir the yellow bean sauce into the pan. When the sauce is hot, add the chicken and then the vegetables and heat through. Serve immediately.

Selections per serving:
½ Fat; 1½ Protein; 2 Vegetable; 50 Optional Calories

(*V*) **Vegetarian option:**
Substitute marinated tofu for the chicken. Reduce the Protein Selections to 1 per serving and reduce the total Calories to 145 per serving.

Honey and Mustard-crusted Pork

Serves 4

Preparation time: 5 minutes
Cooking time: 20 minutes
Calories per serving: 280

Freezing not recommended

**This recipe is a great way to
jazz up grilled meat quickly.**

4 teaspoons sunflower oil
1 tablespoon wholegrain
  mustard
2 teaspoons runny honey
1 oz (30 g) fresh white
  breadcrumbs
4 × 4 oz (120 g) pork loin steaks

1. Preheat the grill. Mix together the oil, mustard, honey and breadcrumbs.
2. Grill the pork under a moderate heat for 8–10 minutes. Turn it over and cook the second side for 5 minutes. Remove the grill pan from the heat, spread the breadcrumb mixture over the pork and return the pan under the grill for 3–5 minutes or until the pork is cooked through and golden. Serve immediately.

Selections per serving:
1 Fat; 3 Protein; 30 Optional Calories

Pasta and Grains

Grains and pasta are an ideal basis for substantial, healthy and delicious meals. ⊛ Rice is the staple food for about half of the world's population, and, like pasta, it is infinitely versatile, easy to cook, convenient and nutritious. ⊛ Two Carbohydrate Selections is equal to a fair-sized portion of pasta or rice. ⊛ There are plenty of recipes with vegetarian alternatives to choose from, such as Creamy Ham, Garlic and Soft-cheese Pasta Ribbons and the tasty Fish Risotto.

Spicy Vegetable and Pine Kernel Pilaf

Serves 4

Preparation time: 10 minutes
Cooking time: 30 minutes
Calories per serving: 395

Freezing not recommended

𝒱

1 tablespoon sunflower oil
2 teaspoons cumin seeds
1 teaspoon turmeric
2 teaspoons garam masala
1/4–1/2 teaspoon paprika
1 large onion, chopped finely
2 garlic cloves, crushed
1 red chilli, de-seeded and
    chopped finely
1 tablespoon grated ginger
2 carrots, peeled and sliced
1 red pepper, de-seeded and diced
1 green pepper, de-seeded and
    diced
1/2 cauliflower, broken into
    small florets
8 oz (240 g) button
    mushrooms, sliced
8 oz (240 g) basmati rice
1 1/2 pints (900 ml) boiling
    water
2 oz (60 g) raisins
1 oz (30 g) pine kernels, toasted
1 tablespoon chopped fresh
    coriander
salt and freshly ground black
    pepper

To garnish:
lemon wedges
fresh coriander

1. Heat the oil and cook the cumin seeds for 1 minute. Mix the turmeric and garam masala with 2 tablespoons of water. Add this to the pan and cook for 1 minute. Then add the paprika, onion, garlic, chilli, ginger, carrots and peppers and stir-fry for 5 minutes.
2. Mix in the cauliflower, mushrooms, rice, water and raisins. Bring to the boil, then reduce the heat and simmer, covered, for 20 minutes. Stir in the pine kernels, coriander and seasoning and serve with lemon wedges, garnished with the fresh coriander.

Selections per serving:
2 Carbohydrate; 1 Fat; 1/2 Fruit; 3 Vegetable; 30 Optional Calories

Tomato and Courgette Rice Bake

Serves 4

Preparation and cooking time:
1 hour
Calories per serving: 305

Freezing not recommended

𝒱 If using free-range eggs
and vegetarian Cheddar
cheese

2 teaspoons sunflower oil
1 onion, chopped
2 large garlic cloves, crushed
1 red pepper, de-seeded and
    chopped
2 courgettes, chopped
6 plum tomatoes, skinned and
    chopped
7 oz (210 g) cooked long-grain
    rice
4 eggs, beaten
1 teaspoon dried thyme
2 oz (60 g) Cheddar cheese,
    grated
1 oz (30 g) fresh white
    breadcrumbs
salt and freshly ground black
    pepper

1. Heat the oil in a frying-pan and gently cook the onion, garlic and red pepper for 5 minutes. Add the courgette, cover the pan and cook for 8 minutes, or until the courgette has softened.
2. Preheat the oven to Gas Mark 4/180°C/350°F. Remove the pan from the heat and stir in the tomatoes, rice, eggs, thyme and seasoning. Spoon the mixture into an ovenproof dish.
3. Mix together the cheese and breadcrumbs and sprinkle them over the rice mixture. Bake for 30–40 minutes or until set and golden.

Selections per serving:
1/2 Carbohydrate; 1/2 Fat; 1 1/2 Protein; 2 1/4 Vegetable; 25 Optional Calories

Fish Risotto

Serves 4

Preparation and cooking time:
30 minutes
Calories per serving: 400

Freezing not recommended

2 tablespoons olive oil
1 leek, chopped finely
2 garlic cloves, crushed
4 oz (120 g) baby button
  mushrooms
8 oz (240 g) risotto rice
4 tablespoons white wine

1½ pints (900 ml) boiling
  vegetable stock
12 oz (360 g) small courgettes,
  sliced
12 oz (360 g) skinless cod fillet,
  diced
1 tablespoon chopped fresh
  basil
4 teaspoons low-fat spread
salt and freshly ground black
  pepper
fresh basil, to garnish

1. Heat the oil in a large saucepan and cook the leek, garlic and mushrooms over a high heat for 3 minutes or until the mushrooms are golden.
2. Stir in the rice, wine and stock. Bring to the boil and simmer for 10 minutes. Add the courgettes and continue to cook for 8 minutes, then add the fish and cook for 2–3 minutes until cooked through. Stir in the basil, low-fat spread and seasoning, and serve immediately, garnished with basil.

Selections per serving:
2 Carbohydrate; 2 Fat; 1 Protein; 1¾ Vegetable; 25 Optional Calories

Variation:
Sprinkle 1 teaspoon of grated parmesan cheese over each portion. This will provide an additional 10 Optional Calories per serving.

Macaroni Cheese with Cauliflower

Serves 4

Preparation and cooking time:
40 minutes
Calories per serving: 520 with reduced-fat cheese; 610 with Cheddar cheese

Freezing recommended

V **If using vegetarian low-fat Cheddar cheese**

I am a great lover of both cauliflower and macaroni cheese; however, a whole bowl of macaroni cheese will use up a lot of Carbohydrate Selections. By combining the two, you get a bulky and delicious meal which fits easily into the Weight Watchers Programme.

8 oz (240 g) macaroni or other
  pasta shapes
1 large cauliflower, broken into
  florets
1 pint (600 ml) skimmed milk
4 tablespoons cornflour
2–3 teaspoons prepared English
  mustard
8 oz (240 g) reduced-fat
  Cheddar cheese, grated
salt and freshly ground black
  pepper

1. Cook the macaroni in a saucepan of fast-boiling salted water for 10 minutes or until tender to the bite, then drain well. Meanwhile, steam the cauliflower above the pasta, or cook in a separate pan of boiling water until just tender, then drain well.
2. Pour a little of the milk into a pan and stir in the cornflour to form a smooth paste. Gradually whisk in the remaining milk. Slowly bring to the boil, stirring frequently until the sauce has thickened. Stir in the mustard, half the cheese and seasoning to taste.
3. Preheat the oven to Gas Mark 6/200°C/400°F. Remove the pan from the heat and stir in the pasta and cauliflower until coated.
4. Spoon the mixture into a large ovenproof dish or four individual ovenproof serving dishes and sprinkle over the remaining cheese. Bake for 15–20 minutes or until golden and bubbling. Serve immediately.

Cook's note:
Wholewheat pasta is ideal for this dish.

Selections per serving:
2 Carbohydrate; ½ Milk; 2 Protein; 1¼ Vegetable; 30 Optional Calories

Pasta with Pepper, Basil, Tomato and Ricotta

Serves 4

Preparation and cooking time:
40 minutes
Calories per serving: 360

Freezing not recommended

V If using vegetarian
parmesan cheese

The addition of ricotta cheese
to this rich, tomato-based
sauce gives it a delicious
creamy taste.

4 teaspoons olive oil
1 large onion, chopped
1 garlic clove, crushed
1 green pepper, de-seeded and chopped
1 red pepper, de-seeded and chopped
1 yellow pepper, de-seeded and chopped
2 × 14 oz (420 g) canned chopped tomatoes
3 tablespoons tomato purée
8 oz (240 g) rigatoni or penne pasta
2 tablespoons chopped fresh basil
4 oz (120 g) ricotta cheese
2 tablespoons grated parmesan cheese
salt and freshly ground black pepper
fresh basil leaves, to garnish

1. Heat the oil and cook the onion and garlic for 5 minutes, then add the chopped peppers and cook for a further 5–8 minutes until softened.
2. Stir in the tomatoes, tomato purée and seasoning and simmer, covered, for 20 minutes.
3. Meanwhile cook the pasta in a saucepan of fast-boiling salted water for 10 minutes or until tender to the bite, then drain well.
4. Stir the drained pasta, basil and ricotta cheese into the sauce and serve immediately, sprinkled with the parmesan and garnished with fresh basil leaves.

Selections per serving:
2 Carbohydrate; 1 Fat; 1/2 Protein; 4 1/2 Vegetable; 15 Optional Calories

Creamy Ham, Garlic and Soft-cheese Pasta Ribbons

Serves 4

Preparation and cooking time:
15 minutes
Calories per serving: 340

Freezing not recommended

The low-fat soft cheese gives
this dish a really delicious
creamy sauce which tastes as
though it is full of Calories!
For a special occasion I
substitute the ham with
smoked salmon.

8 oz (240 g) tagliatelle tomato/ spinach
8 oz (240 g) low-fat soft cheese with garlic and herbs
5 tablespoons skimmed milk
2 oz (60 g) lean ham, cut into strips
salt and freshly ground black pepper

1. Cook the pasta in plenty of fast-boiling salted water for 10 minutes or until tender to the bite.
2. Meanwhile stir together the cheese and milk in a large saucepan until smooth. Heat gently and stir in the ham. Remove the pan from the heat.
3. Drain the pasta thoroughly, then add it to the pan of cheese and ham and toss thoroughly. Return to the heat and warm through. Season to taste and serve immediately.

Selections per serving:
2 Carbohydrate; 1 1/2 Protein; 5 Optional Calories

(V) Vegetarian option:
Substitute 1 lb (480 g) steamed broccoli florets for the ham. This will reduce the Protein Selections to 1 per serving and will give 1 Vegetable Selection per serving and 345 Calories per serving.

Tuna, Courgette and Leek Lasagne

Serves 4

Preparation time: 10 minutes
Cooking time: 1 hour
Calories per serving: 435

Freezing recommended

2 teaspoons vegetable oil
1 onion, chopped
2 garlic cloves, crushed
1 leek, chopped finely
14 oz (420 g) canned chopped
  tomatoes
2 tablespoons tomato purée
2 courgettes, halved lengthways
  and sliced

1 teaspoon dried oregano
8 oz (240 g) canned tuna in
  brine, drained and flaked
4 oz (120 g) pre-cooked lasagne
  sheets
4 oz (120 g) mature Cheddar
  cheese, grated
salt and freshly ground black
  pepper
For the white sauce:
4 teaspoons margarine
1 oz (30 g) plain flour
1/2 pint (300 ml) skimmed milk
1 teaspoon prepared English
  mustard

1. Heat the oil in a pan and cook the onion, garlic and leek for
5 minutes or until softened. Stir in the tomatoes, tomato purée,
courgettes and oregano. Bring to the boil, then reduce the heat,
cover the pan and simmer gently for 15 minutes.
2. Meanwhile, prepare the white sauce. Melt the margarine in a
saucepan, then stir in the flour and cook for 1 minute. Gradually
whisk in the milk and cook, whisking continuously, until the sauce
thickens. Remove the pan from the heat, stir in the mustard and
season well.
3. Preheat the oven to Gas Mark 5/190°C/375°F. Stir the tuna and
seasoning into the tomato sauce. Spoon half of the tuna mixture
into an ovenproof shallow dish and top with half of the lasagne
sheets. Then spread over half of the white sauce and sprinkle with
half of the cheese. Repeat the layers in the same order to use up the
remaining ingredients, finishing with a sprinkling of cheese.
4. Bake for 35 minutes until bubbling and golden brown.

Selections per serving:
1 Carbohydrate; 1 1/2 Fat; 1/4 Milk; 2 Protein; 3 Vegetable;
20 Optional Calories

Mixed Mushroom Pasta

Serves 4

Preparation time: 10 minutes
Cooking time: 35 minutes
Calories per serving: 470

Freezing not recommended

V **If using vegetarian
margarine and Cheddar cheese**

8 oz (240 g) pasta
4 teaspoons sunflower
  margarine
2 garlic cloves, chopped
4 oz (120 g) baby button
  mushrooms

6 oz (180 g) chestnut closed-
  cup mushrooms, quartered
6 oz (180 g) small open-cup
  mushrooms, sliced
1 teaspoon dried rosemary
2 tablespoons plain flour
1/4 pint (150 ml) skimmed milk
12 oz (360 g) low-fat (up to 8%)
  fromage frais
2 oz (60 g) Cheddar cheese,
  grated
salt and freshly ground black
  pepper
chopped fresh parsley, to
  garnish

1. Cook the pasta in fast-boiling salted water for 10 minutes or
until tender to the bite. Drain well.
2. Meanwhile heat the margarine in a frying-pan and cook the
garlic, mushrooms and rosemary for 10 minutes over a low heat.
Season to taste.
3. Stir in the flour and cook for 1 minute, then gradually stir in the
milk, stirring continuously until the mixture thickens.
4. Preheat the oven to Gas Mark 5/190°C/375°F. Remove the pan
from the heat and transfer the mixture to a large ovenproof dish.
Stir in the drained pasta and then the fromage frais and seasoning.
5. Sprinkle over the Cheddar cheese and bake for 20 minutes or
until bubbling. Serve immediately, garnished with a sprinkling
of parsley.

Selections per serving:
2 Carbohydrate; 1 Fat; 2 Protein; 1 1/4 Vegetable; 25 Optional
Calories

Puddings, Cakes and Biscuits

With the flexible Weight Watchers Programme there is no reason why you can't indulge in puddings and still lose weight. ✳ This chapter is packed full of tantalising treats from the luscious hot baked Pear and Raspberry Nutty Crumble and a Spicy Apple Strudel to delectable fruity numbers such as Apricot Mousse, Raspberry and Hazelnut Pavlova and a rich and creamy Orange and Sultana Cheesecake. ✳ The scrumptious Fruity Flapjacks and Cinnamon Biscuits are ideal for curbing the appetite when you crave sweet food!

Baked Fruits in Foil

Serves 4

Preparation time: 10 minutes
Cooking time: 12 minutes
Calories per serving: 90

Freezing not recommended

V

These fruit parcels are simple to make and release a delicious aroma when opened, revealing warm, lightly poached fruits.

2 × 4 oz (120 g) bananas
4 oz (120 g) strawberries, halved
1 medium orange, peeled, halved and sliced
1 medium peach, peeled, stoned and sliced
juice and zest of 1 medium orange
1 teaspoon Sweetex sweetener
sprigs of fresh mint, to decorate

1. Preheat the oven to Gas Mark 6/200°C/400°F.
2. Peel the bananas and halve them lengthways. Place each half in the centre of a square piece of foil and scatter over the strawberries, orange slices and peach slices. Spoon the orange juice and zest over the fruits.
3. Bring the two edges of foil together to encase the filling, forming a parcel, and fold the edges to seal. Place the parcels on a baking sheet and bake for 10–12 minutes.
4. Open up the parcels, sprinkle with the sweetener and serve immediately, garnished with the mint sprigs.

Selections per serving:
1½ Fruit

Apricot Mousse

Serves 6

Preparation time: 10 minutes + 30 minutes chilling
Cooking time: 10 minutes
Calories per serving: 200

Freezing not recommended

V **If using free-range eggs**

8 oz (240 g) ready-to-eat dried apricots
6 fl oz (180 ml) water

6 cardamom pods, crushed lightly
12 oz (360 g) low-fat (up to 8%) fromage frais
zest and juice of 1 medium orange
10 fl oz (300 ml) low-fat natural yogurt
2 egg whites
1 medium orange, peeled and segmented
fresh mint, to decorate

1. Place the apricots and water in a saucepan and stir in the cardamoms. Bring the mixture to the boil, then reduce the heat and simmer for 10 minutes or until the apricots are soft. Remove the pan from the heat.
2. Remove the cardamom pods from the apricots and discard them. Place the apricots and liquid, fromage frais and orange juice in a food processor or blender and process until smooth.
3. Transfer the mixture to a bowl and fold in the yogurt and orange zest.
4. Whisk the egg whites until stiff but not dry, and fold them into the apricot mixture.
5. Roughly chop the orange segments and fold them into the mixture. Spoon the mixture into individual ramekin dishes and chill for at least 30 minutes before serving. Decorate with fresh mint.

Selections per serving:
1½ Fruit; ¼ Milk; 1 Protein; 25 Optional Calories

Raspberry and Hazelnut Pavlova

Serves 4

Preparation time: 15 minutes
Cooking time: 1½ hours
Calories per serving: 245

Freezing not recommended

V **If using free-range eggs**

2 egg whites
4 oz (120 g) caster sugar
¾ teaspoon white wine vinegar
¾ teaspoon vanilla essence
1 teaspoon cornflour
1 oz (30 g) shelled hazelnuts, chopped
1 teaspoon oil, for greasing
For the filling:
6 fl oz (180 ml) Total light greek yogurt
8 oz (240 g) raspberries
2 kiwi fruit, peeled, halved and sliced

1. Whisk the egg whites until stiff. Gradually whisk in the sugar and continue to whisk until glossy, then whisk in the vinegar, vanilla essence and cornflour. Finally, fold in the nuts very carefully.
2. Preheat the oven to Gas Mark 2/150°C/300°F. Pile the mixture on a greased baking sheet lined with baking parchment and spread it out to form a circle about 7 inches (18 cm) wide. Hollow out the centre slightly. Bake for 1½ hours, then allow to cool.
3. Fill the centre with the greek yogurt and top with the fresh fruit. Serve immediately.

Cook's note:
Of course any other fruit can be substituted for the raspberries and kiwi fruit. Strawberries and paw paw are also delicious.

Selections per serving:
1 Fat; 1 Fruit; 180 Optional Calories

Spicy Apple Strudel

Serves 4

Preparation time: 20 minutes
Cooking time: 20 minutes
Calories per serving: 255

Freezing not recommended

V **If using vegetarian margarine**

Spicy apple puddings are my favourite so this creation is a real winner for me – it tastes really rich and wicked!

1 lb (480 g) cooking apples, peeled, cored and sliced
zest and juice of ½ lemon
zest of ½ orange
½ oz (15 g) low-calorie Sucron sweetener
a pinch of grated nutmeg
1 teaspoon ground cinnamon
2 oz (60 g) sultanas
3 oz (90 g) filo pastry sheets, thawed if frozen
3 tablespoons margarine, melted
1 oz (30 g) soft white breadcrumbs
1 teaspoon oil, for greasing
½ teaspoon icing sugar

1. Place the apple slices in a bowl and toss them in the lemon juice. Mix in the lemon and orange zest, sweetener, spices and sultanas.
2. Unwrap the filo pastry, and overlap the sheets on a tea towel to give a 12-inch (30 cm) square, brushing the layers with the melted margarine as you go. Brush the whole surface with the margarine.
3. Sprinkle the breadcrumbs over the surface, leaving a 1½-inch (4 cm) border around the whole edge.
4. Spoon the apple mixture over the breadcrumbed surface. Fold two parallel sides of pastry in by 1½ inches (4 cm) to form the ends of the strudel and brush the pastry with the margarine. Then, from one of the unfolded edges, roll up the strudel like a swiss roll, using the tea towel as a guide.
5. Preheat the oven to Gas Mark 5/190°C/375°F. Transfer the strudel to a greased baking sheet lined with baking parchment and brush the strudel all over with the remaining melted margarine.
6. Bake for 20 minutes or until crisp and golden. Serve hot, sprinkled with the icing sugar.

Cook's note:
Low-calorie Sucron is a sugar alternative that works well in cooking as the granules are a blend of sugar and saccharin.

Selections per serving:
1 Carbohydrate; 2 Fat; 1½ Fruit; 20 Optional Calories

Pear and Raspberry Nutty Crumble

Serves 4

Preparation time: 10 minutes
Cooking time: 40 minutes
Calories per serving: 325

Freezing recommended

V If using vegetarian margarine

Pears and raspberries are a fantastic combination which proved very popular with all my tasters!

1 lb (480 g) firm, ripe pears, peeled, cored and sliced
1 tablespoon lemon juice
8 oz (240 g) raspberries
1 tablespoon Sweetex sweetener
For the topping:
2 oz (60 g) plain flour
1½ oz (45 g) sunflower margarine
2 oz (60 g) porridge oats
1 oz (30 g) flaked almonds
1 oz (30 g) demerara sugar

1. Preheat the oven to Gas Mark 4/180°C/350°F.
2. Toss the pears in the lemon juice and then mix in the raspberries and sweetener. Spoon the mixture into an ovenproof dish.
3. Place the flour in a bowl and rub in the margarine. Stir in the oats, almonds and sugar and sprinkle the mixture over the fruit.
4. Bake for 35–40 minutes or until golden brown.

Selections per serving:
1 Carbohydrate; 2 Fat; 1½ Fruit; 75 Optional Calories

Fruity Yogurt Brûlée

Serves 4

Preparation and cooking time:
20 minutes
Calories per serving: 350

Freezing not recommended

V

12 oz (360 g) ready-to-eat mixed dried fruit (i.e. apple rings, apricots, pitted prunes, figs, sultanas, pear)
8 fl oz (240 ml) red wine

8 fl oz (240 ml) water
zest and juice of 1 medium orange
zest and juice of ½ lemon
8 cloves
a pinch of ground nutmeg
1 cinnamon stick
2 tablespoons Sweetex sweetener
10 fl oz (300 ml) low-fat natural yogurt
4 teaspoons demerara sugar

1. Place the fruit in a saucepan with the wine, water and zest and juice of the orange and lemon. Stir in the spices.
2. Bring to the boil and simmer for 10 minutes until the fruit is tender. Remove the pan from the heat and stir in the sweetener.
3. Preheat the grill. Spoon the fruit with a little of the juice into four flameproof serving dishes. Place a spoonful of yogurt over each pile of fruit.
4. Sprinkle over the sugar and place the dishes under the grill for a few minutes until bubbling and caramelised.

Selections per serving:
2 Fruit; ½ Milk; 145 Optional Calories

Orange and Sultana Cheesecake

Serves 6

Preparation time: 10 minutes
Cooking time: 40 minutes
Calories per serving: 255

Freezing not recommended

$\mathcal{V}$ **If using free-range eggs
and vegetarian margarine and
curd cheese**

**This cheesecake has such a
delicious, rich, creamy texture
that no one ever believes that
it can be eaten on the Weight
Watchers Programme!**

For the base:
2 tablespoons margarine
2 oz (60 g) rich tea biscuits,
    crushed (approximately 7
    biscuits)
For the filling:
8 oz (240 g) curd cheese
2 oz (60 g) caster sugar
2 eggs, separated
7 oz (210 g) low-fat (up to 8%)
    fromage frais
zest of 1 orange
juice of 1/2 medium orange
1 oz (30 g) sultanas

1. Lightly grease a 6½-inch (17 cm) loose-based cake tin and line
the base with baking parchment. Melt the margarine and mix in
the crushed biscuits. Press the mixture into the base of the tin.
2. Beat the cheese, sugar and egg yolks until smooth. Then fold
in the fromage frais and the orange zest, orange juice and the
sultanas.
3. Preheat the oven to Gas Mark 3/170°C/325°F. Whisk the egg
whites until stiff but not dry, and very carefully fold them into the
cheese mixture until everything is completely blended. Pour over
the biscuit base.
4. Bake the cheesecake for 40 minutes or until risen and just firm
to touch. Leave to cool in the tin and then chill.

Selections per serving:
1 Fat; 1½ Protein; 155 Optional Calories

American Muffins

Makes 12

Preparation time: 10 minutes
Cooking time: 25 minutes
Calories per muffin: 195

Freezing not recommended

$\mathcal{V}$ **If using free-range eggs
and vegetarian margarine**

10 oz (300 g) plain flour
1 tablespoon baking powder
1/2 teaspoon salt
3 oz (90 g) caster sugar
zest of 1 lemon
3 oz (90 g) sultanas
2 eggs, beaten
8 fl oz (240 ml) skimmed milk
2 oz (60 g) sunflower margarine
1/2 teaspoon icing sugar

1. Sift the flour, baking powder and salt into a mixing bowl. Stir in
the sugar, lemon zest and sultanas.
2. Beat together the eggs, milk and margarine. Make a well in the
centre of the dried ingredients and pour in the liquid.
3. Preheat the oven to Gas Mark 6/200°C/400°F. Stir the mixture
gently to form a batter (do not worry if it remains lumpy as over-
mixing spoils the final texture).
4. Spoon the mixture into a 12-hole non-stick muffin tin and bake
for 20–25 minutes until golden and risen. Allow to cool on a wire
rack. Serve while still slightly warm, sprinkled with icing sugar.

Cook's note:
If you don't have a non-stick tin you can line the tin with paper
muffin cases.

Selections per muffin:
1/2 Carbohydrate; 1 Fat; 90 Optional Calories

Fruity Flapjacks

Makes 16

Preparation and cooking time: 25 minutes
Calories per flapjack: 175

Freezing not recommended

V If using vegetarian margarine

These deliciously filling treats are naturally sweetened with honey and dried fruits.

4 oz (120 g) sunflower margarine
4 tablespoons light runny honey
8 oz (240 g) oats
1½ tablespoons wholemeal flour
1 teaspoon baking powder
2 oz (60 g) sultanas
2 oz (60 g) ready-to-eat dried apricots, chopped
1 tablespoon sesame seeds
1 oz (30 g) flaked almonds
1 teaspoon oil, for greasing

1. Preheat the oven to Gas Mark 5/190°C/375°F.
2. Melt the margarine and honey in a saucepan, then remove the pan from the heat and stir in the remaining ingredients.
3. Spoon the mixture into a lightly greased 8-inch (20 cm) baking tin and press down firmly with the back of a metal spoon.
4. Bake for 20 minutes or until golden. Mark into 16 squares while still hot, then leave to cool and harden in the tin. When completely cold, cut the flapjack into squares and store them in an airtight container.

Selections per flapjack:
½ Carbohydrate; 1½ Fat; 45 Optional Calories

Cinnamon Biscuits

Makes 16

Preparation time: 10 minutes
Cooking time: 15 minutes
Calories per biscuit: 70

Freezing recommended

V If using vegetarian margarine and free-range eggs

2 oz (60 g) margarine
1½ oz (45 g) caster sugar

1 egg, separated
3½ oz (105 g) plain flour
a pinch of salt
½ teaspoon ground mixed spice
½ teaspoon ground cinnamon
1 oz (30 g) currants
1 tablespoon milk
1 teaspoon granulated sweetener, for sprinkling

1. Cream the margarine and sugar until pale and fluffy, then beat in the egg yolk. Sift in the flour, salt and spices and mix well.
2. Add the currants and the milk, and mix to form a soft dough.
3. Preheat the oven to Gas Mark 6/200°C/400°F. Knead the dough lightly, then roll it out on a lightly floured surface and cut out 16 rounds using a 2½-inch (6 cm) fluted pastry cutter.
4. Place the biscuits on a baking sheet lined with baking parchment and bake for 10 minutes.
5. Take the biscuits out of the oven, brush them with the egg white, sprinkle over the sugar and return them to the oven for 5 minutes until golden.
6. Transfer the biscuits to a wire rack to cool. Once cold, store them in an airtight container.

Selections per biscuit:
½ Fat; 50 Optional Calories

Snappy Storecupboard Suppers

This chapter contains a variety of snacks, meals and desserts made from store-cupboard ingredients, making use of canned beans and fish, commercial sauces in jars, and sachets of low-calorie chocolate drinks. ⊗ There is even a crunchy topping for ice cream made from nuts, breadcrumbs and sugar.

Tuna and Lemon Pâté

Serves 4

Preparation time: 5 minutes
Calories per serving: 200

Freezing not recommended

This pâté is really quick to make and I often have it for lunch with Melba toasts or wholemeal toast and a salad garnish.

8 oz (240 g) canned tuna in brine, drained and flaked
4 tablespoons Weight Watchers from Heinz low-calorie mayonnaise
lemon juice, to taste
salt and freshly ground black pepper
1 oz (30 g) Melba toasts or wholemeal toast

1. Place the tuna in a small bowl with the mayonnaise and mash with a fork. Alternatively place the tuna and mayonnaise in a food processor and process until smooth.
2. Mix in the lemon juice and seasoning to taste and serve with Melba toasts or wholemeal toast.

Selections per serving:
1 Carbohydrate; 1½ Fat; 1 Protein

Paprika Bean Casserole

Serves 4

Preparation and cooking time: 35 minutes
Calories per serving: 325

Freezing recommended

𝒱

2 teaspoons sunflower or olive oil
2 large onions, quartered and sliced

1 garlic clove, crushed
14 oz (420 g) canned whole red pimientos, drained and chopped
12 oz (360 g) canned cannellini beans, drained and rinsed
2 tablespoons paprika
2 × 14 oz (420 g) canned chopped tomatoes
2 tablespoons tomato purée
8 oz (240 g) rice or couscous

1. Heat the oil in a large saucepan and cook the onions and garlic for 5 minutes.
2. Stir in the pimientos, beans, paprika, tomatoes and tomato purée. Bring to the boil, then cover the pan and simmer for 25 minutes.
3. Meanwhile cook the rice or couscous according to the directions on the packet.
4. Spoon the rice or couscous on to four serving plates and top with the casserole. Serve immediately.

Selections per serving:
2 Carbohydrate; ½ Fat; 1 Protein; 3½ Vegetable

Spicy Yogurt-topped Minced Lamb

Serves 3

Preparation and cooking time:
55 minutes
Calories per serving: 355

Freezing not recommended

6 oz (180 g) lean minced lamb
295 g jar of Weight Watchers
    from Heinz Mexican Chilli
    Cooking Sauce
¹/₂ pint (300 ml) water
6 oz (180 g) closed-cup
    mushrooms, sliced
1¹/₂ oz (45 g) raisins
10 fl oz (300 ml) low-fat
    natural yogurt
3 oz (90 g) mature Cheddar
    cheese, grated

1. Cook the minced lamb in a non-stick pan until browned and drain off any excess fat, then stir in the sauce, water, mushrooms and raisins and bring to the boil. Reduce the heat and simmer for 15–20 minutes.

2. Preheat the oven to Gas Mark 5/190°C/375°F. Spoon the mixture into an ovenproof dish. Beat together the yogurt and cheese. Spread the yogurt mixture over the minced lamb and bake for 30 minutes or until the yogurt has set.

Selections per serving:
¹/₂ Fruit; ¹/₂ Milk; 2 Protein; 1 Vegetable; 60 Optional Calories

(*V*) **Vegetarian option:**
Substitute 6 oz (180 g) minced Quorn for the minced lamb. Do not dry-fry the Quorn: simply mix it in a saucepan with the sauce and then heat through. Use vegetarian Cheddar cheese. This will reduce the Optional Calories to 40 per person and the Calories per serving to 310.

Crunchy-topped Strawberries and Ice Cream

Serves 4

Preparation and cooking time: 10 minutes
Calories per serving: 180

The crunchy topping for this recipe is really moreish and can be made in advance and kept in an airtight container.

1 oz (30 g) shelled hazelnuts, chopped finely
1 oz (30 g) wholemeal breadcrumbs
1½ teaspoons demerara sugar
4 oz (120 g) strawberries, sliced
10 oz (300 g) Weight Watchers from Heinz vanilla ice cream

1. Preheat the grill. Mix together the hazelnuts, breadcrumbs and sugar on a baking sheet. Place it under a moderate grill for about 5 minutes, stirring frequently, until the mixture is crisp and golden. Allow to cool.
2. Divide the strawberry slices between four stemmed glasses and spoon over the ice cream. Sprinkle over the crispy nutty mixture and serve immediately.

Cook's note:
Of course you can use other fruits, e.g. 4 oz (120 g) sliced banana or
4 oz (120 g) raspberries.

Selections per serving:
1 Fat; 140 Optional Calories

White Chocolate Custard Pots

Serves 4

Preparation and cooking time: 40 minutes + 30 minutes chilling
Calories per serving: 85

Freezing not recommended

½ pint (300 ml) skimmed milk
2 sachets Options white chocolate drink powder
2 eggs, beaten
a pinch of grated nutmeg or ground cinnamon

1. Pour the milk into a saucepan and heat gently until almost boiling. Whisk in the sachets of Options powder.
2. Pour the milk mixture on to the beaten egg, stirring to blend. Strain the mixture into four small ramekins.
3. Preheat the oven to Gas Mark 3/170°C/325°F. Place the ramekins in a roasting tin and pour in enough boiling water to come halfway up the sides of the ramekins.
4. Sprinkle the custards with nutmeg or cinnamon, then bake them for 30 minutes or until just set.
5. Remove the ramekins from the roasting tin, allow them to cool and then chill them in the refrigerator for at least 30 minutes before serving.

Selections per serving:
¼ Milk; ½ Protein; 30 Optional Calories

Basic Sauces and Dressings

The last chapter gives a selection of basic sauces and tasty salad dressings. ⊗ There is a cheese sauce and a rich tomato sauce, which are useful recipes to have to hand, as they both appear in many dishes such as lasagne and cauliflower cheese. ⊗ I have also given a recipe for a deliciously tangy barbecue sauce which really jazzes up grilled and barbecued meat or makes a great jacket potato topper. ⊗ Salads can be transformed into something really delicious when they are completed with a dressing. ⊗ However, many dressings have a high proportion of oil which can make them disastrous for the waistline. ⊗ I have created two dressings which fit in with the Programme without skimping on flavour. ⊗ Lastly, for all chocolate addicts, I had to include an irresistible hot chocolate sauce to be poured over ice cream or fresh fruit.

Cheese Sauce

Serves 4

Preparation and cooking time: 15 minutes
Calories per serving: 215 (with half-fat Cheddar 170; with Stilton 215)

𝒱 **If using vegetarian Cheddar cheese**

4 tablespoons cornflour
1 pint (600 ml) skimmed milk
4 oz (120 g) mature Cheddar cheese, grated
1–2 teaspoons English mustard
salt and freshly ground black pepper

A simple and quick cheese sauce which is delicious simply poured over cooked pasta, steamed vegetables or toast.

1. Place the cornflour in a saucepan and gradually whisk in the milk.
2. Heat the milk mixture, stirring continuously until the sauce boils and thickens. Reduce the heat and simmer gently for 2–3 minutes.
3. Stir in the cheese, mustard and seasoning and heat through gently.

Cook's note:
Half-fat Cheddar cheese can also be used in this sauce, or other types of cheese such as Stilton.

Selections per serving:
½ Milk; 1 Protein; 30 Optional Calories

Rich Tomato Sauce

Serves 4

Preparation and cooking time: 35 minutes
Calories per serving: 35

𝒱

1 teaspoon sunflower or olive oil

1 large onion, chopped
1–2 garlic cloves, crushed
2 × 14 oz (420 g) canned chopped tomatoes
2 tablespoons tomato purée
salt and freshly ground black pepper

1. Heat the oil in a saucepan and gently cook the onion and garlic for 5 minutes, or until softened.
2. Stir in the tomatoes, tomato purée and seasoning. Bring to the boil, then simmer for 20–30 minutes, or until thickened.

Selections per serving:
3 Vegetable; 10 Optional Calories

Variations:
Creamy Tomato Sauce: Purée the sauce in a food processor or blender with ¼ pint (150 ml) skimmed milk until smooth. Return to the saucepan and heat through. Remember to add 10 Optional Calories per person. The total Calories per serving will be 50.
Basil and Tomato Sauce: Stir in 2 tablespoons of freshly chopped basil just before serving. The total Calories per serving will be 35.

Barbecue Sauce

Serves 4

Preparation and cooking time: 25 minutes
Calories per serving: 65

V If using vegetarian margarine

This sauce is a particularly good accompaniment to barbecued food. During the winter months it is a great way to spice up plain grilled meats.

2 tablespoons margarine
1 onion, grated
2 tablespoons tomato purée
2 tablespoons malt vinegar
2 teaspoons mustard powder
2 tablespoons Worcestershire sauce
2 tablespoons Sweetex sweetener
1/4 pint (150 ml) water

1. Stir together all the ingredients in a saucepan and slowly bring to the boil. Reduce the heat and simmer for 20 minutes, or until thick.

Selections per serving:
1 1/2 Fat; 1/4 Vegetable

Fromage Frais and Herb Salad Dressing

Serves 4

Preparation time: 5 minutes
Calories per serving: 55

V

4 oz (120 g) low-fat (up to 8%) fromage frais
2 tablespoons Weight Watchers from Heinz low-calorie
mayonnaise
1 tablespoon lemon juice
1 teaspoon chopped fresh parsley
1 tablespoon chopped fresh chives
salt and freshly ground black pepper

1. In a small bowl blend together the fromage frais and mayonnaise. Stir in the remaining ingredients and season to taste.

Selections per serving:
1/2 Fat; 1/2 Protein; 10 Optional Calories

Blue Cheese Dressing

Serves 4

Preparation time: 5 minutes
Calories per serving: 115

V If using vegetarian Stilton

2 oz (60 g) Stilton cheese, grated
5 fl oz (150 ml) low-fat natural yogurt
1 tablespoon sunflower oil
1/2–1 teaspoon lemon juice
salt and freshly ground black pepper

1. Mix together the cheese and yogurt in a small bowl. Slowly stir in the oil and lemon juice. Season to taste.

Selections per serving:
1/2 Fat; 1/4 Milk; 1/2 Protein; 10 Optional Calories

Hot Chocolate Sauce

Serves 4

Preparation and cooking time:
5 minutes
Calories per serving: 95

V

A delicious sauce to pour over vanilla ice cream or fresh fruit.

1 teaspoon cocoa powder, sifted
2 teaspoons cornflour, sifted
1/4 pint (150 ml) skimmed milk
2 oz (60 g) plain chocolate, chopped
3 tablespoons Sweetex sweetener

1. Place the cocoa powder and cornflour in a small saucepan and slowly whisk in the milk to avoid any lumps.
2. Add the chocolate to the pan and slowly bring the mixture to the boil, stirring continuously to form a smooth, thick sauce. Stir in the sweetener and serve immediately.

Selections per serving:
95 Optional Calories

Index

Herb salad dressing, fromage frais and **74**
High-fibre salad **6**
Honey and mustard-crusted pork **46**
Horseradish cottage pie, beef and **36**
Hot chocolate sauce **76**

Ice cream, crunchy-topped strawberries and **70**
Italian-style stuffed pancakes **18**

Kebabs, cod and prawn **40**
Kidney beans, red:
　Rich bean moussaka **38**
Lamb:
　Grilled lamb with minted yogurt **40**
　Spicy yogurt-topped minced lamb, **68**
Lasagne, tuna, courgette and leek **54**
Leeks:
　Cheese, leek, tomato and basil flan **28**
　Tuna, courgette and leek lasagne **54**
Lentil soup, orange and **14**

Macaroni cheese with cauliflower **50**
Mackerel pâté, peppered smoked, with wholemeal toast **12**
Mediterranean-style salad, roasted pepper **8**
Meringue:
　Raspberry and hazelnut Pavlova **58**
　Mexican stir-fry pancakes **42**
　Minced lamb, spicy yogurt-topped **68**
Mixed mushroom pasta **54**
Moussaka, rich bean **38**
Mousse, apricot **56**

Mozzarella bread-stick pizza, speedy tomato, bacon and **24**
Muffins, American **62**
Mushrooms:
　French-bread toasts **10**
　Mixed mushroom pasta **54**
　Open-crust chicken and mushroom pie **26**
Mustard bread pudding, cheese and **16**
Mustard-crusted pork, honey and **46**

New potato, spinach and feta frittata **16**

Open-crust chicken and mushroom pie **26**
Orange and lentil soup **14**
Orange and sultana cheesecake **62**

Pancakes:
　Italian-style stuffed pancakes, **18**
　Mexican stir-fry pancakes, **42**
Paprika bean casserole **66**
Parcels, baked fish **30**
Parcels, salmon **28**
Pasta:
　Creamy ham, garlic and soft-cheese pasta ribbons, **52**
　Macaroni cheese with cauliflower **50**
　Mixed mushroom pasta **54**
　Pasta with pepper, basil, tomato and ricotta **52**
　Tuna, courgette and leek lasagne **54**
Pasta sauces:
　Creamy ham, garlic and soft-cheese **52**
　Mixed mushroom **54**
　Pepper, basil, tomato and ricotta **52**

Pâtés:
　Peppered smoked mackerel pâté with wholemeal toast **12**
　Tuna and lemon pâté, **66**
Pavlova, raspberry and hazelnut **58**
Pear and raspberry nutty crumble **60**
Peppers, sweet:
　Pasta with pepper, basil, tomato and ricotta **52**
　Roasted pepper Mediterranean-style salad **8**
　Stuffed baked peppers **34**
Peppered smoked mackerel pâté with wholemeal toast **12**
Pies:
　Beef and horseradish cottage pie, **36**
　Open-crust chicken and mushroom pie, **26**
　Steak and kidney pie, **26**
Pilaf, vegetable and pine kernel, spicy **48**
Pizzas:
　Speedy tomato, bacon and mozzarella bread-stick pizza **24**
　Tasty tuna and prawn pizza **24**
Pork:
　Honey and mustard-crusted pork **46**
　Pork, prune and apple stew **36**
Potatoes:
　Baked chips **34**
　Beef and horseradish cottage pie **36**
　Creamy haddock and prawn potato bake, **32**
　Fish cakes, baked **30**
　Haddock, egg and cheese baked potatoes **22**

New potato, spinach and feta frittata **16**
Potato and broccoli soup **14**
Potato, prawn and avocado salad **6**
Prawns:
　Cod and prawn kebabs, **40**
　Creamy haddock and prawn potato bake, **32**
　Mexican stir-fry pancakes **42**
　Potato, prawn and avocado salad **6**
　Tasty tuna and prawn pizza, **24**
Prune and apple stew, with pork **36**
Pudding, cheese and mustard bread **16**
Purée, avocado **42**

Quorn:
　Fragrant Quorn, spinach and tomato curry *(V)* **32**
　Quorn and horseradish cottage pie *(V)* **36**
　Spicy yogurt-topped Quorn *(V)* **68**
Raspberries:
　Pear and raspberry nutty crumble **60**
　Raspberry and hazelnut Pavlova **58**
Red kidney beans:
　Rich bean moussaka **38**
Relish, tomato **42**
Rice:
　Fish risotto **50**
　Rice salad in blue cheese dressing, chicken and **10**
　Spicy vegetable and pine kernel pilaf **48**
　Tomato and courgette rice bake, **48**
Rich bean moussaka **38**
Rich tomato sauce **72**
Risotto, fish **50**

Roasted pepper Mediterranean-style salad **8**
Root vegetables, creamy baked **20**

Salads:
Chicken and rice salad in blue cheese dressing **10**
High-fibre salad **6**
Potato, prawn and avocado salad **6**
Roasted pepper Mediterranean-style salad **8**
Salmon parcels **28**
Sauces:
Barbecue sauce **74**
Basil and tomato sauce **72**
Cheese sauce **72**
Creamy tomato sauce **72**
Hot chocolate sauce **76**
Rich tomato sauce **72**
Spicy tomato sauce **42**
Soft cheese, with pasta ribbons, creamy ham, garlic and **52**
Souffléd tuna-stuffed tomatoes, cheesy **20**

Soups:
Creamy cheese and vegetable soup **12**
Orange and lentil soup **14**
Potato and broccoli soup **14**
Speedy tomato, bacon and mozzarella bread-stick pizza **24**
Spicy apple strudel **58**
Spicy tomato sauce **42**
Spicy vegetable and pine kernel pilaf **48**
Spicy yogurt-topped minced lamb **68**
Spinach:
Fragrant chicken, spinach and tomato curry **32**
New potato, spinach and feta frittata **16**
Steak and kidney pie **26**
Stew, pork, prune and apple **36**
Stir-fries:
Chinese fish stir-fry, **44**
Chow mein stir-fry, **44**
Crunchy chicken stir-fry, **46**
Mexican stir-fry pancakes, **42**

Strawberries and ice cream, crunchy-topped **70**
Strudel, spicy apple **58**
Stuffed baked peppers **34**
Stuffed pancakes, Italian-style **18**

Tasty tuna and prawn pizza **24**
Toasts, mushroom french-bread **10**
Toasts, tomato garlic **8**
Tofu, crunchy stir-fry *(V)* **46**
Tomatoes:
Basil and tomato sauce **72**
Cheese, leek, tomato and basil flan **28**
Cheesy souffléd tuna-stuffed tomatoes **20**
Creamy tomato sauce **72**
Fragrant chicken, spinach and tomato curry **32**
Pasta with pepper, basil, tomato and ricotta **52**
Rich tomato sauce **72**
Speedy tomato, bacon and mozzarella bread-stick pizza **24**

Spicy tomato sauce **42**
Tomato and courgette rice bake **48**
Tomato garlic toasts **8**
Tomato relish **42**
Tuna:
Cheesy souffléd tuna-stuffed tomatoes **20**
Tasty tuna and prawn pizza **24**
Tuna and lemon pâté **66**
Tuna, courgette and leek lasagne **54**

Vegetable and pine kernel pilaf, spicy **48**
Vegetable soup, creamy cheese and **12**
Vegetables, root, creamy baked **20**

White chocolate custard pots **70**

Yogurt:
Fruity yogurt brûlée, **60**
Grilled lamb with minted yogurt **40**
Spicy yogurt-topped minced lamb **68**